MW00889742

☑ Enable Better Service

A Customer Service Contact Center Story of Breaking Away from the Norm Through Creativity, Technology and Innovation.

Aarde Cosseboom

ISBN-13: 9 781798 035818

ISBN-13+5: 9 781798 035818 90000

Edition 1.4 190408

Published by Amazon Kindle Direct Publishing

This book is dedicated to the contact center leaders of the world; to enable them to create better customer experiences by utilizing best business practices.

CONTENTS

INTRODUCTION: The Future of Contact Centers

1. The Service Onion

2. Gas up for the Long Customer Journey

3. Soft-Serve your way to Self-Service

4. Get off the Ground - Live in the Clouds

5. Tortilla Chips and Data Dips - Smart Routing Techniques to Save any Party

6. Pick a Partner not a Vending Machine

7. The Best Defense is a Good Offense - More than a Cost Center

8. LLTV - Key to Long-lasting Life Time Value

9. Creating a Frictionless Experience - Key to Customer Effort

10. WFM and Staffing Practices gone Wild – The Power of One

11. Know your Customers Multiple Personality Profiles – Persona Based Routing

12. The Subjective vs. Objective Spectrum

13. Scorecard Stretch Goals and Benchmarking Performance

14. Foster Employee Drive – Performance-Based Pay

15. Customer Experience is based off Employee Experience

16. Photocopy your Best Talent - Re-recruit your A Players

ACKNOWLEDGEMENTS

APPENDIX

ABOUT THE AUTHOR

Enable Better Service

FORWARD

Have you ever heard someone rave about amazing customer service? That OMG moment that really highlights how someone went out of their way to help someone. The real question is; was this experience organic and just happened because the service representative was just "that good" or was it previously engineered through contact center strategy? There are times where we, as customer service leaders, can get lucky with hiring the right people, train and equip them perfectly, and hope that the right service moment strikes. Often times these can hit like bolts of lightning, sharp and intense, but often never hitting the same spot again... or at least in a predictable manner. What if there were ways that we could engineer these experiences and leverage tools and technology to help lightning strike every single time. Think of it like the lightning rod on the top of the Empire State Building in Manhattan, which gets hit by lightning about 23 times per year. That lightning rod was engineered to direct the lightning through the rod and channel it safely all of the way down the building to the ground. Without this rod a high percentage of those lightning strikes could and would be dangerously uncontrolled.

Wayne Gretzky, arguably the best hockey player in the history of the NHL, once said "you miss 100% of the shots you don't take." Even though Gretzky is only ranked 43rd in highest Shooting Percentage with an amazing 894 goals out of 5088 shots (17.57%), he is a great example of how someone who can be well known without being the best. This is exactly how NPS (Net Promoter Score) works for our world. Getting an amazing word of mouth referral is like gold, or in the Wayne Gretzky's example it's like getting a key sponsorship or winning the 1990s Athlete of the Decade award. How did he do it; was it just luck mixed with a little skill? Gretzky honed his skills as a kid at a backyard rink and regularly played minor league hockey at a level far above his peers. He took shot after shot against older and larger kids' day in and day out, mostly loosing, just to gain the experience needed to get better. Some may say that this is training, but to me this is more similar to environmental engineering. He created a physical environment for himself to grow and get better, challenging himself after every missed shot/opportunity. Creating that environment where he could eventually allow lightning to strike (or goals in this example) over and over again. While this was done with physical conditioning he also grew up in a place that allowed for him to go outside and take these shots day in and day out. If he lived in a warm climate like Florida, this might not have been possible. Remember that we, as customer service leaders, have the ability to influence the environment and create the best possible experiences.

You may be asking yourself; how do we have the opportunity to engineer this for our teams and companies? I purposely used the word "we" in the question above to point out that you are not alone. You won't find all of the answers in this book, but it is here to spark healthy debate and possibly plant the seed to help you and your teams succeed in creating a better customer experience through customer service for everyone to benefit from. I invite you and your teams to use this book as a tool to calibrate with, deliberate over, and even argue with. I challenge you to start a book club, mark this up with highlighters, whiteboard ideas and workflows. I recommend that you challenge the content in this book, it is not the absolute answer and isn't for every company or team. All that I hope is for this book to enable you and your team to be armed with something to show to your Executives to help push the world's customer service to the next level. Just like Gretzky did to shatter those NHL records and the Engineer who designed the lightning rod on the top of the Empire State Building for the sole purpose of saving lives.

Lightning can be engineered to hit the same spot more than twice and goals can happen a higher percentage of time with a well-planned tool and the right people. If you take anything from this book it is that a well-engineered team is made up from engineering the right **People, Process, and Product.** "I never commit to memory anything that can easily be looked up in a book." Albert Einstein. This are wise words to live by. Remember that there is no need to memorize these ideas, but rather read and reflect on how you could potentially leverage them to better serve your customers.

If you find yourself trying to turn the pages of this book to find the answers, you might find yourself with more questions than answers. That is ok, remember the title of John C. Maxwell's book - *Good Leaders Ask Great Questions.* Questions help you learn, learning drives innovation and positive change. I invite you to embrace this method and leverage it to gain some advantages across your business. Turn the page and get your notepad out to write down those questions and get one step closer to Enabling Better Service.

INTRODUCTION:

The Future of Contact Centers

Not everyone looks forward to calling a contact center. Most people don't pick up the phone and smile from ear to ear in anticipation for that "press 1 for…" and "average wait time is 2 minutes." For those select few that oversee a contact center you may actually enjoy calling in so that you can listening to see if there is some way you can glean how other contact centers are providing their service. When I call in, I try to be as perceptive as possible when I need to interact with a company that I'm a consumer of. Whether over the phone, email, chat, through a bot or even finding the answer myself via some help articles there are always ways to check out how others are surprising and delighting their customers.

Contact centers are complex and often an afterthought for some companies. This is especially apparent for companies that grow quickly and are in the most need of an efficient way to answer customer's questions. When there is hyper growth for a company it is easy for a non-efficient contact center to grow in a way that becomes costly and sticks out like a sore thumb on the bottom line. Commonly these contact centers are labeled as **cost centers** and are quickly asked to cut budget. There are ways to combat this misconception and turn your contact center into a well-oiled machine that can also save the bottom line. Thinking outside of the box will not only save the perception of the team but it will also help get you closer to your company's financial goals. Here are just a few topics we will cover in this book; profit center, deflection with self-service and bots, and maximizing team productivity.

You might have heard of a little company called Amazon. As you might know already, they have a vast variety of product spanning from a thriving online ecommerce marketplace to manufacturing their own electronics. They even can deliver groceries and food directly to your door. What you might forget is that they started with the simple idea to digitize books. Eliminating the need for the bookstore, publishers, etc. Even with this expansive enterprise, dare I say monopoly (I hope my Alexa isn't hearing this as I write the draft of this book) they have always delivered amazing support. Another area they excel is delivering new and innovative support channels. You might not notice it, but they focus on delivering service though the lowest cost channels (even for the most complex of issues). If you have an issue with a grocery purchase or delivery you can file a case through the Amazon Prime app and get a response within minutes. If you didn't notice, these are delivered with Bots that offer things like $5 off your next purchase, using a Machine Learning algorithm to qualify if you are a valuable customer or not. This is a cost-effective way to provide amazing service with little to no interaction with an actual customer service representative. They also have a very well-engineered Contact Us Page that qualifies your question first and tries to provide self-service if applicable. It will also suggest the appropriate support channel (phone, chat, email) for the question/issue that you might have. This not only pushes contact volume to properly staffed areas of the support team, but also allows you to choose your channel preference. It's like a choose your own adventure book, but for support. Sounds like a win/win to me.

Mayday... Mayday... I need support ASAP! Another way Amazon disrupted the contact center space was with the Mayday Button on all of their tablets and eReaders (Kindles). This was a FaceTime like experience that allowed the end user to see and hear a support representative with a click of a button. Although it never really took off it was a huge step forward in innovation and created buzz in the contact center space. Another innovative channel that Amazon has developed is the push to talk button on their Amazon Fire TV Sticks. This integrates their Alexa Voice technology to help you self-serve the issues you have with your other Amazon devices. The example here is that you might see an error on your Amazon Fire TV Stick, instead of calling, chatting, or emailing support you can just press the button and pull up a community forum or FAQ article. Now we all don't have the ability to enable these channels and features into our products, but it is just another innovative way to help people help themselves.

Amazon is such a well-known brand that even some of the younger generations have Googled this; "Is the Amazon river owned by Amazon.com?" They are obviously doing something right, and their customer service strategy mirrors this.

Take a second to think about how your contact center is setup today. Can you innovate? Does it need innovation? How hard would it really be? How many months/years/decades are you from being able to implement something that is truly innovative? Now before you start to say those contrarian phrases in your head, truly think about how you can get your company to this new bar. Because before you know it, all of your competitors will have self-service bots, AI and utilize Machine Learning and start to win the race against you in becoming an efficient (cost and service) customer experience machine.

Over the last decade I have dedicated my professional career to help my companies in these endeavors. Innovating with CRM *data dips*, smart routing, AI bots, integrated self-service tools within product, and Machine Learning. What I have learned is that if you have the right employees, vision, partners and technology it isn't that hard to implement positive changes rather quickly. Removing roadblocks and aligning with the correct vendors and employees is truly how to get off the ground and into the clouds. This is where the contact center is going, and it is going to get there fast! Don't be left behind. There might be a time in the near future where future generations will never have to pick up the phone, initiate a chat, or send an email to get support. When was the last time you sent a physical letter to someone requesting support for something? That is where the current aging channels are going... the way of the dinosaur. Only the companies that will offer support in the way that their customers are actually looking for will survive. This might not be the way we think of it today. The future of support may very well not include Phone or Chat. There might more trendy methods in our near future.

If you haven't read *The Effortless Experience* by Matthew Dixon, Nick Toman, and Rick DeLisi I highly recommend it. It frames up the idea that the future of support is providing answers to the customers via their preferred channel with as little complexity as possible. For example, most people don't like to read long FAQs for simple issues. They also have an amazing introduction that highlights how some companies like the Ritz-Carlton and Zappos are creating *"Blinded by Delight"* customer experiences. Although both examples in their book are more mechanical than automated, we can take those examples and try to apply them to automated systems through AI, Bots and Machine Learning.

One of the ways I have done this at my current company is by creating a retention Chat and Voice Bot that utilizes Machine Learning AI to retain customers.

These Bots are designed to offer the best endowment ($xx dollars off of next purchase) based off of customer value and segmentation. Since it is in the cloud we can leverage AI to recalculate both dollar amount and confidence rate for possible retention. I dig a little deeper into how this works and is setup in future chapters so stay tuned. The future of support and contact centers is already upon us. Some innovative companies have already crossed the chasm and implemented key initiatives to reduce the bottom line. It's important to stay ahead of the curve and possibly even be a trailblazer.

1

The Service Onion

Most people in the contact center customer service industry don't go home for the holidays bragging to their elders about their jobs. The topic of Contact Centers and support over the phone (at least in the western culture) is never regarded very highly. You often don't see kids responding to the age-old question; "What do you want to be when you grow up?" with something like, "I want to manage a call center."

But while we don't have the most attractive, dare I say 'sexy', jobs in the world we make up for it by helping people with literally everything they need. Almost every industry needs contact centers to help better service their customers. Some companies have tried to sell products with little to no support options and they ultimately loose out to their competitors that have support channels. Don't forget some of the most valuable industries to our economy. For example; health care industry, State and Federal services (including 911 and 211 suicide hotlines) where they literally save lives! There are less critical companies that provide great support to products like video games, entertainment and shopping. No matter where you are on the spectrum, support has its value to your organization.

What most people don't know is that there are

layers to supporting customers and it goes beyond the traditional 1-800 phone numbers. I'm not only talking about email, chat, social, SMS, and all of those other channels. I am referencing the hidden secret levels of service that we all use every day without even noticing. If done right these self-service education and self-service automation layers can not only help you deflect volume into your contact center, but they can also empower the next generation of customers with tools to self-serve.

What is *The Service Onion*? The best way to describe it is to quote the classic 2001 Dreamworks film *Shrek*.

Shrek: "Ogres are like onions."

Donkey: "They stink?"

Shrek: "Yes. No."

Donkey: "Oh, they make you cry."

Shrek: "No."

Donkey: "Oh, you leave em out in the sun, they get all brown, start sproutin' little white hairs."

Shrek: "No. Layers. Onions have layers. Ogres have layers. Onions have layers. You get it? We both have layers."

Donkey: "Oh, you both have layers. Oh.

You know, not everybody like onions."

Customer service is no different. If not done correctly they create really bad customer experiences and you might get reviews in your CSAT surveys saying that your service "stinks." If you don't have a successful way of deflecting contacts, you might have to hire large numbers of staff members to handle the volume and that will make you "cry." If you don't update your technology you might have to deal with long and difficult service interruptions or issues, much like letting your onion sit out in the sun to brown and start sprouting "hairs." If you do it just right you can setup layers of support that help with all of these potential issues, turning you from an ugly ogre of a contact center into the Knight that saves the day.

Before we dig further into the Service Onion, first put your customer "hat" on. OK, you just bought a new dog house and need to assemble it. What is the first thing you would do? Read the instruction manual? Watch a YouTube video on how other people assembled it? Ask a neighbor? Call or email the company and ask for step by step options? You might decide to start with something like, read the manual (self-help documentation), then if you got stuck you might go watch a YouTube video. But it is very unlikely you would call the manufacturer or send them an email. Although you may not be the company that needs to support assembly of dog houses, you can replace this scenario with your product(s) and ask the same questions. Try to really put the customers "hat" on. Really role play this out or you won't truly be able to think outside the box (the box being traditional phone, email, chat channels). If it is hard for you to go through this exercise, try surveying your existing customers or pull together a customer focus group. Another great way to do this is to ask new hires (people who just started at your company) to help answer these questions.

Once you have a list of possible service channels and self-help solutions put them together as if they were layers of an onion. See *Figure 1.1* below for an example of a *Service Onion*.

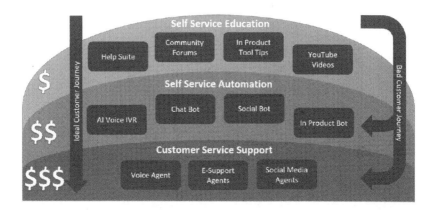

Figure 1.1 The Service Onion – Layers of Self-Service

As you can see from the example, you can have multiple layers to your support. The outer layers are usually the least costly as they can be done with free services like YouTube or it can be static Help Suites or

FAQs. You can have user generated support content that can be managed and maintained in Community Forums or embed tool tips and videos within your product (helpful if you have a digital product, website, app, etc.). Most of these solutions have a low MRC (Monthly Recurring Cost) due to the ability to scale quickly with crowd sourcing and very little, to no need, for one to one responses from a contact center team member.

Often companies will forget or neglect to create the second layer of the onion. This is the new trend in the customer service space and is catching on quickly. This layer is the Self- Service Automation layer. This is commonly known as the AI (Artificial Intelligence), Machine Learning, automation bot layer. Tools like Chatbots and Automated Voice IVRs can help pull up information, process simple tasks, and even schedule callbacks and create cases on your behalf without the need to talk to a team member. I have used these extensively throughout my career in multiple different flavors and they have been proven to be extremely successful with customer satisfaction and contact deflection. Saving the company money and keeping customers loyal and happy. Sounds like a win/win solution to me. If you are not doing this today or haven't looked into technology to help with this area, you are missing the bus. There are small boutique companies that can make very custom builds for your needs along with large companies that can give you something out of the box to help with simple level 1 transactional inquiries; like surfacing FAQs while in chat or resetting a password.

AI and Machine Learning is the future of customer service. Today the middle layer is hard to perfect, and achieve with success, without some heavy manual setup and direction. This is changing by the year, dare I say month. As vendors are perfecting their offerings, these options are becoming easier to implement and more cost effective. Being an early adopter to this new technology wave will bring huge returns while other companies are learning to adapt. There are plenty of vendors in this space that are willing to put extra effort in co-designing these bots with your company in an effort to stay relevant and ahead of their completion. Some specialize in languages, while others focus on specific service channels. At this time, I have found it beneficial to partner with multiple vendors to support a truly global and multi-channel environment of AI bots. That environment might change as one of the trailblazers of this area emerges. If you have a specific need (like an AI IVR Voice Bot) I recommend shopping around and finding a partner that fits your requirements. You might want to ask if your vendor is flexible or rigid in their development AI flows as that was a huge part of our vendor selection process for these tools. I cover this in more detail in upcoming chapters so stay tuned.

As the technology starts to grow and get better to support this middle layer we will see it squeeze its way into the first and third layer. Potentially replacing the usage and volume to self-service tools like a community forum and static help guides. This is because the AI bots will provide faster answers then a community of peers and can use Machine Learning to adapt answers to be more customized then an older published help guide articles. I believe that AI will eventually replace the need for tier 1/2 type questions that are being answered by traditional channels today (phone, chat and email). Potentially completely replacing a 1 to 1 support channel like phone in the more distant future. Google is working on a technology that acts like a personal assistant for consumers for simple tasks like; reserving a table at a restaurant to setting up a salon appointment. In the near future we will have bots doing the same on the customer service side, utilizing this same technology and Machine Learning. In the near future we might actually witness AI bots marking and receiving these calls. Meaning that no actual human will have part of the conversation from both consumer or the company. For companies that don't adapt to these changes we might see an increase in self-serviceable contacts from AI personal assistants on behalf of your customers. This could cause a very lopsided technology gap between the way that consumers and companies communicate to each other. Potentially creating very costly support environments that support inexpensive customer engagement options.

If the future of customer support and contact centers truly is in the AI realm, how will you prepare?

What can you do now to make sure you're ready to start using AI when the time comes? An important part of AI is the engine that runs behind it. Most partners have their own preparatory Machine Learning engine driving their product. These algorithms can either live in the cloud (multiple business cases utilizing the same engine), be setup in segmented cloud, or on-premise databases (locally hosted). The thing they all have in common is; the more data you put through it the more it learns from itself. Some vendors piece together different tools and custom setups to create the AI that best fits your needs. For example; having an AI Voice product that is completely cloud (shared across multiple businesses) and Machine Learning that is segmented based off of your brand or company. What this does is allows for the AI Voice to learn new words and phrases, while your call flow only changes based off of previous volume going into your company. This prevents other businesses unique setups to affect your call flows in any way. See *Figure 1.2* below for an example of this architecture.

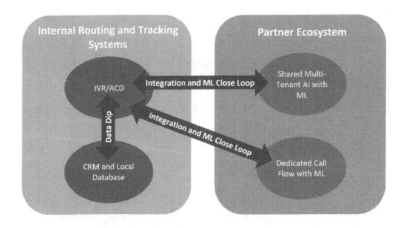

Figure 1.2 AI and Machine Learning Partner Ecosystem

Machine Learning is something that you can do internally as a company instead of using a vendor/partner. You can also have this setup independently from your AI Bots by configuring it to give you valuable information about your customers and creating something similar to a LTV (Life Time Value) score. Machine Learning tools can be purchased and configured to take an array of data points from your CRM, IVR and other data sources to output and evaluate your customers before making a decision. This LTV score is extremely valuable to help route your customers based off of value. *Bullseye routing* is a technique you can use once you have these scores in place. See *Figure 1.3* for an example of bullseye routing.

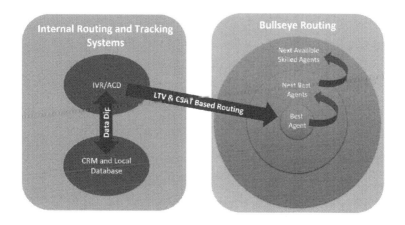

Figure 1.3 Bullseye Routing

An example of this is when you have a high value customer and a high performing agent. You of course want to route the most valuable customers to the agent that has the highest quality. If they are not available, you could route to the next highest quality agent(s). Repeating this until the customer is connected to someone. In this example you would send the data (who the customer was routed to) back into the Machine Learning algorithm with success KPIs (quality metrics) to help the Machine Learning learn from itself. Even if you don't have a high repeat caller scenario (this also works for all other channels like chat and email) the Machine Learning algorithm will put a value on the customer calling in and value them as if they were a repeat caller. This is based off of previous callers with similar attributes. This helps predict the outcome of what will happen in these interactions. Once you have enough data feeding into this closed loop ecosystem you can run simulations based off of average LTV score customers and average Quality scores of the team. Allowing you to calculate COD (Cost of Delivery) when your environment changes over time. For example: your marketing department launches a product where your LTV of customer is lower (a cheaper product) you can plug that into this simulation and prove with numbers that you don't need to hire high quality team members to support this lower value segment of customers. Another option is to route this segment to your newer/lower quality agents. Another example of how to use this simulation is to calculate LTV based off of matching your valuable customers to lesser quality agents. An example of this would be; a highly seasonal call center that has huge volume around a holiday. Let's say Valentine's Day and the product is flowers. You know that you can hire large amounts of high quality agents during your February month. You might have to settle for a higher quantity of agents over higher quality. If you can calculate or forecast this drop in overall quality, you can reverse engineer potential drop in LTV due to this and justify the decision to hire lower quality agents.

Even though I might not have added it to the figures above, there might be other similar tools within this layer that can fall into this category. An example of one that has been around for a while is SMS two-way authentication. This is often used by banks to ensure that you are who you say you are when trying to reset a password to something as sensitive as a mortgage brokerage account or your checking account. Another great example of a tool that falls into this category is using *data dips* when callers call in to pull up stored billing information, past purchase history and other member information that can be used to self-serve or smart route to the appropriate support representative(s).

The third, and most costly, layer is the traditional customer service support channels that we all know very well; phone, email, chat, social, SMS, etc. While these are still valuable channels they can be very costly. Even if you have mainly chat or social where you can scale your team members efficiently due to the ability to service multiple customers at once. Even with gained efficiency here, you are still most likely going to spend more money providing that manual level of support instead of self-service channels in outer layers. I deduce that this layer is the highest cost per contact, but it is important to note that some companies and customers prefer this channel and you should never truly try to remove it. Unless you're sure your customers don't need/want it. For example: some people will always (at least for now) want to call a restaurant to ask questions or leave a reservation, even though there are self-service options like Yelp or OpenTable to help with that. Your most loyal and valuable customers might prefer these channels and would switch to one of your competitors if these channels were to go away or have a worse perceived level of support with high wait times. Some of this is generational, while some of it is preference. Either way, it is important to know your customer base and adapt to their desires.

Once you have your layers in place you should do *customer journey mapping* to help visualize how your customers are being serviced within this onion. There are companies that help consult or have tools that monitor these behaviors, but if you want to go low tech you can do something as simple as grabbing a sample set of your customers and following them through this process. As I mentioned earlier, a great way to do this is to have new hires buy your product and record their experience as they try to self-serve or get support. Like an internal secret shopper. At one of my previous companies we actually had the CEO do this monthly and reported the customer journey experience in town hall meetings to articulate how we supported the brand behind our products. It was a lot like that CBS TV show *Undercover Boss*, but without all of the wigs and cameras.

You might not have the ability to pull in Executives from your company to do some secret shopping and help with the customer journey. If you don't (even though I highly recommend you try to get them to commit to this) you can also go very low tech. Shadowing and side by side listening of calls in real time is one of the best ways to get the customer experience. I have heard from other companies that they buy old iPods and load them up with contact center recorded calls. Hand them out to executives and ask for them to listen in to these calls while they commute into work or are working out. This is a good way to have Executives hear and listen to what their customers are saying and asking on a daily basis. You don't have to select good/bad/short/long calls, it is actually better to just have these randomly selected so they can be unfiltered and raw.

Now that you know more about *the service onion*, how will you use it to embrace the next generation of AI and Machine Learning? Are you a company that needs to lean in and embrace it or do your customers prefer traditional support (Phone, Email, Chat, etc.)? Are your customers skipping layers of the onion by choice? Should they be? Do they even know about the first two layers? These are all questions you should try to answer before exploring these different layers. Truly digest this information and come up with a high-level game plan before it's too late. I recommend asking yourself these questions regularly (annually or biannually) to reassess where you are and where you want to be as a company.

If you are having difficulty answering these questions you can always ask your customers what they would prefer. But be cautious as they might not even know what they want. They may be apprehensive to have a bot helping them solve their issues (as most people would be). Do you think people wanted a self-checkout kiosk at the grocery store before they used one for the first time? Or being able to order your Starbucks from your mobile app before getting to the store? Maybe not. These are examples of physical queues of people and how these companies used self-service automation to create better experiences. Henry Ford - inventor of the first motorized vehicle, the Model T; once said, "If I had asked people what they wanted, they would have said faster horses." At first the Model T wasn't popular, people were afraid of sitting on a mechanical device that had a gas tank (highly flammable) strapped to it. Back then there weren't gas or fuel tanks on mobile transportation devices, everything was powered by coal and horse. This is a great example of when innovation needed to be tested and proven to be able to change the way customer interact and utilize a product. If you were to ask your customers today; "What kind of customer service do you want?" You probably would get the same response, "faster answer time and resolving my issue the first time." You probably would not get people asking for an automated system to help them resolve their issue without having to talk to a human. Although with the newer generations this has started to change. Younger generations want/expect self-service and self-service automation. Think Uber, Air Bnb, and Amazon. As a consumer of these products I would rarely expect to talk to a real live human to resolve my issues (unless absolutely necessary). If I need support or have an issue, I just open their apps and submit a ticket. Within minutes I will get an email back with information. These usually have an agents name attached, but often times are just responded to by an automated bot with a coupon code off of my next purchase. The future of AI, Machine Learning, and automation is here and if you aren't in the Model T you are stuck with your old horse drawn carriage.

2

Gas up for the Long Customer Journey

Childhood years are often a distant memory. There are several events and trips that stick out in my mind from those early years of my life. One of those experiences turned my summer vacation from boring, sitting on the coach all summer, into a journey of a lifetime. I was about 13 and just finishing up one of my middle school years. With some already experienced travel already under my belt, due to being rewarded with a family trip every year if I got good grades (which I always got), I wasn't too excited that we were going on a road trip instead of our usual Caribbean Cruise or week in Hawaii.

One day after getting home from school my Dad pulled me into the yard and showed me a camper shell that he had just bought. If you are not familiar with a camper shell they are like a studio apartment that you put on the back of your pickup truck. They have a loft bed that overhangs the front of the truck cab and usually have a small kitchenette and small bathroom. I don't specifically remember if it had a shower. If you are really lucky there is a little breakfast nook (table) that converts into a small twin bed, this area was my home for the summer. This was sometime in the 1990s and my family preferred to be cost effective with trips. This family adventure was not only cost effective but allowed us to really bond and make memories. This was a clear difference from the trips I had gone on in previous year; with the all you can eat buffets, fun cruise ship kid's activities, and lunches/dinners on the beautiful Hawaiian island watching whales and turtles frolicking in the shallow shores. Even with those initial selling point setbacks, I was determined to make the best of it.

As my Dad proudly showed me his newly purchased camper shell we walked around it and carefully checked all of it gadgets and gizmos. These would truly enable us to have a great family journey. I was in charge of helping him line up his 1980s something Chevrolet truck as he slowly backed it into position so that we could lower the camper shell and tie everything down. Later in my life I came to realize that he was teaching me how to be prepared for launching large scale projects. Not only mentally prepared, but how to make sure everything is prepared from a product standpoint. I take this process very seriously today when launching new contact center and technology products for the team. Much like loading up the camper shell, launching a new Chatbot or Quality Monitoring process has to be carefully monitored and planned to go successfully. No rock or gadget left unturned or tested. Else it would create a horrible customer journey, and in this example a horrible family vacation.

In a time before smartphones and GPS, the only

way for us to navigate this epic journey was via maps. I clearly remember the foldable maps that we got from our AAA insurance company in years past. I was lead navigator, and as a boy scout I took this job very seriously. Imagine days of planning with maps, highlighters, pens, and pencils all scattered on the living room coffee table as if a tornado hit a craft store. This was what I would equate to as a RFI/RFP process that most companies do today. The level of detail that I went through in this process was mindboggling. From picking out bathroom stops, notable landmarks we wanted to visit, down to calculating potential gas station stops to *gas up* along the way. I can't take all, or really most of the credit here as I was a little too young to fully plan out the family adventure, my parents helped out immensely with the planning process.

As I loosely mentioned in the Forward of this book I truly believe that the key to any successful business is rooted in a strong focus on **People, Process, and Product.** I put these in order of what I think is most important. If I didn't have the right **People** (my Mom and Dad), **Process** (maps and planned preparedness for the trip), and **Product** (Camper Shell that fits the whole family and 2 dogs) we would not have succeeded in having a thriving business (Family trip). Caution; You can have two of these three in place and still horribly fail at what you are trying to accomplish. My advice is to pick and hire the right **People**, do all of the necessary work to make sure you **Process** is sound, and truly take your time purchasing or creating the right **Product**. Don't cut corners or settle for anything less than near perfect for all of these areas. See *Figure 2.1* by Han van Loon below to help utilize these tools to your advantage.

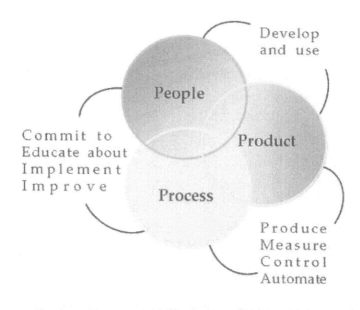

Figure 2.1 People Product and Process

I would be remised to say that this is **all** you need to create a great customer journey. Just like my family vacation, there are issues and roadblocks that may come up that really test this system. Even with hours/days/months of planning the perfect setup, things can still go horribly wrong. This is the same for family vacations and customer journeys alike. Although nothing went horribly wrong on our family vacation around the

United States South West, things most certainly could have. From possibly running out of gas, to having to drive long hours during the night with the majority of the family asleep and unable to keep the driver awake or on the right navigational path. The contact center is no different. Things like shrinkage can force you to be drastically short staffed when you need the team the most. Natural disasters and power outages can catch your contact center off guard without a sound contingency plan in place. These all affect the customer journey. Even with a single poor experience the whole journey can be skewed into a lower total customer satisfaction (CSAT) result.

On this particular family trip, I remember enjoying the hot sun beating down on us as we dipped our feet into the clear blue water of Lake Powell. By this time, we were halfway through our month-long journey and we wanted nothing more than a cleansing dip in this picturesque lake. I vividly remember the shelves of sandstone that we would walk down (as if huge human formed steps were placed there purposely). This was the obvious high point of the trip. Much like the customer journey we try to provide our customers every day. This is exactly how the customer journey goes, there are peaks and valleys of satisfaction. Times where you get to experience the best and not so best experiences. See Figure 2.2 for examples of how these peaks and valleys might form.

"I've learned that people will forget what you said, people will forget what you did, but people will never forget how you made them feel." Maya Angelou

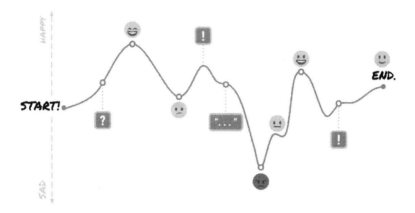

Figure 2.2 Customer Journey and Satisfaction; Justin Owings posted on June 07, 2017. *Customer Journey Maps, Session Replay, and the Power of Empathy.* Retrieved from https://blog.fullstory.com/customer-journey-maps-session-replay-and-the-power-of-empathy/

Although it may seem like this was the quintessential family trip of a young boy's life, there were some low points. I remember stopping at a cheap hotel late one night (after all of the local restaurants were closed) and not having a way to make any dinner. My Dad being the engineer that he was, used the coffee pot to heat up some water so we could make some Top Ramen. Even though we wanted a nice meal, all three of us had to settle for a single pot of warm Top Ramen. This reminds me of those customer experiences that are not so great and cause your customers to really regret committing to you and your product. But at the end of it all, I really enjoyed the trip and wouldn't have traded it for the world.

Customers will remember those low and high points. This is why it is so important to try to keep the experiences as positive as possible. Even though I didn't have to the choice to pick the trip, in your contact center you have the ability to choose who creates these experiences. Choosing someone like by Dad who can think on his feet and create a workaround that creates a great experience out of a horrible situation. It's all about the **People** you staff to represent your company.

When recruiting I like to give my candidates questions that ask how they would troubleshoot a bad experience with some sort of work around or possible solution. We often role-play having them troubleshoot a TV remote that isn't working and ask them how they would help someone with that issue over the phone. We look for customer service team members that start by asking questions like; "Is the TV responding to manual buttons being pushed?" and "Do you see a light when you press the buttons on the remote?" After asking clarifying questions we look for someone who will then try to solve the issue with non-conventional ways. Examples include; "Do you have other TVs in the house where you can switch remotes and retest?" and "Let's try programming a different universal remote to see if it is the remote or the TV not accepting the signal." It's these types of customer service team members that will prevent the reshipping of new remotes that might come at a high cost to the company. These new remotes would also take time to ship that would cause a prolonged bad customer experience. Or even worse, we can waste the time and money to reship the remotes and it can still not solve the issue.

At a very high level it is important to map out your projects to help your team create the best customer journey. This doesn't need to be a high tech project and/or take a very long time. You can and should start by using a whiteboard or notepad to write down the current journey. I recommend you do this with your senior leadership team or other key executives at your company. The goal in this exercise is to figure out where you need to focus your energy on improving the customer journey. Some areas might be quick wins while others might take larger projects or large changes in **Process**. Every time you find a gap in service you might notice that this is where your contact center gets hit with the most questions and concerns. This is where you can start to categorize your issues and try to troubleshoot. If you solve issues up stream, finding the root issue, you might solve more than just one inquiry into the contact center. This can possibly lower overall contacts and deflect unneeded reasons for customers to contact your company, while improving the customer experience.

What is your desired customer journey? What experiences do you want your customers to have when engaging with your support service levels? Do they have a hard time getting to the answer or resolution to their issues? These aren't questions that are easily answered. Often times we have an idea of what a customer wants, but it can always be a little tainted by our own perception. Remember your customers might not be the same. Some may want a quick customer journey, while others want a longer journey. Some customers enjoy the long journey and that is why they went with your product/company.

A great example of this is AAA insurance and Gieco. Gieco likes to advertise "15 minutes can save you 15 percent or more". If every customer wanted that then the other insurance companies would be out of business. Then why do people still have AAA? Although AAA and Gieco don't have the exact same product offerings, they both offer Auto insurance. Why do people still choose AAA for their auto insurance? The answer might surprise you. Yes, some are loyal to their old insurance company, "if it's not, broke why fix it?" Yes, AAA has amazing add-ons like bundling Home and boat insurance. Yes, AAA has roadside assistance packages. The surprising answer is that some people want to talk to people when it comes to insuring some of their most important assets (cars, boats and homes). They don't want to speed up that process. They want to feel like the company on the other side of the phone is investing enough time and energy into building the relationship. This is why AAA wins some of the insurance business. This is what makes them unique.

Focus on your current and prospective customers when trying to plan this journey. Give them options so you don't alienate a portion of your market. Engage with your sales and marketing teams to understand what type of customers you want to target. If the costumer journey is longer and over more costly channels, bake that into your costs and report that back so you don't under budget your contact center. Push back when a market segment might be too costly to support and engage with sales and marketing to potentially bake the support cost into the cost of that new product offering. This is how you can stay ahead and be proactive vs. just reacting to potential changes. This is another way to keep customer service at the top of mind, even in the early planning stages, instead of being an afterthought.

When planning your costumer experience think about the long game. Don't create an experience that cuts your customer's potential lifetime short. If you really put the time and energy into planning individual experiences you will find that customers will be more loyal and stay customers longer. Word of mouth about bad customer experience travels faster than good customer experiences. Keep this in mind when designing the customer experience.

Sometimes too many touch points can be bad. If

you have a product that doesn't need a lot of engagement, it might be best to pare down the emails and proactive communication. Remember that as a contact center you aren't the only department that may be reaching out to the customer. Often times a sales or marketing team will have post sale drip campaigns that will initiate x days after go live. At one of my previous companies we did our journey mapping and found out that we were sending more than 100 emails within the first 30 days. We found that multiple departments were sending emails exactly 30 days post go live. This means that the customer was getting 5 to 10 emails all in one day from the same company (just different departments). Although individual departments had the best of intentions, it actually causes a negative experience when 5 to 10 different departments reached out at the same time. Imagine signing up for Netflix and getting 10 emails 1 month after signing up. How fast would you try to opt out or cancel?

As you can probably tell from my social media, the things in life that inspire me are eating and travel. As you go through this book you will see many references to food and traveling from place to place. This is a passion that is pretty universal among most people, so it can be easily relatable to the mass audience. Although I have never worked in either industry, as a customer, I like to glean from those experiences and incorporate them into my day to day work. I invite you to do the same! Find things that interest you and see how they treat their customers (you). The next time you are out to dinner, visiting a new city, using tools to book/plan your next meal or vacation, focus on the experience. See how they respond with your service needs. See how you can contact them if you have any issues.

I was recently on a trip to Nashville with a US based Airline (shall not be named) where I was accidentally charged for Wi-Fi twice. This had to do with their app not loading when the purchase button was clicked, and I had to use the back button to reset the page. Not necessarily their fault, but I didn't want to be charged twice for Wi-Fi on my 4 hour flight none the less. I went to contact this company and was shocked to find out that I could not email or chat with them. My only channel option was phone. Still being on the plane and not having cell service I found myself getting a little anxious. I had to remind myself to call them when I landed. This would mean I would have to wait on hold during my personal time while in Nashville. Being an introverted millennial, I would have rather just sent an email with a screenshot of my bank statement instead of having to talk to someone and explain the situation. This is the experience I could get when using Amazon or Uber. I forget to mention that the Wi-Fi on this flight was $18, which is $2 more than the cocktail I bought! I really didn't want to pay $36 for 4 hours of Wi-Fi, but I honestly felt like it was more valuable than spending 30 minutes on the phone during my trip. When I finally called it was a 30 min wait time, so I decided not to wait and lose out on my $18 overcharge.

As I was using my Wi-Fi over the duration of the flight I found that every internet issue I had (large or small) would exponentially frustrate me, because I knew I was paying a premium for the service. As pages wouldn't load, as they often do on planes, I found myself frustrated rather than accepting the experience (like I normally would feel in those instances). This might sound a little silly to some, but I landed and started my trip in a mood that was less happy than I should have been. All because I couldn't resolve my issue in the way I wanted to. I ultimately didn't get my double charge resolved but will actively try to fly another airline when I plan my future trips if given the option. This is a great example of a bad customer journey based off of a bad customer experience. If that company just had a self-service or self-service automation tool like a Chabot I would have been a happy customer and probably be a returning customer. I don't recommend booking your flights only based off of what Airline has the right customer service channels and tools, but as a contact center leader you should map these customer journeys from beginning to end and highlight these pain points, so it doesn't happen to your company. If you work for an Airline company and need advice and consulting on this, my name is on the cover, feel free to reach out to me. ;)

Companies are now adopting a new metric to help score these journeys. It is aptly named the Journey

Excellence Score (JES) and measures the overall journey into a 10 point score, 1 – 10. If I were to rank the JES of the Wi-Fi Experience I had with the airline it would probably be about a 2, as a 1 would be a complete failure of finding the way to contact the company. What you want to do is focus on things like customer channel preference and self-service options so that you start off with a high JES right off the bat. Referring back to Figure 2.2 above, customers score you (mentally) based off of experiences and amount of friction it takes to get their issue resolved. Your JES is the collection of all of those experiences over time. Starting off with a positive experience right for their first couple of experiences helps set your company up for success with that customer. Over time they will expect the trend and start giving your company/brand the benefit of the doubt when the experience is less than perfect.

3

Soft-Serve your way to Self-Service

There is an art to serving the perfect swirly cone of soft serve frozen yogurt on the first try. It is even more challenging when you are behind a counter and trying to make one for a customer. If you didn't do it just right, you would have to throw it away and start over again. My first customer service job (technically I didn't get paid so more like an internship) was during summer break of my first two years of high school. I would go to work with my grandma at TCBY in SFO - San Francisco International Airport. TCBY (The Countries Best Yogurt) was a frozen yogurt chain back in the 90s that was one of the few businesses in the soft serve yogurt market at the time. This was a time long before the self-service frozen yogurt shops you see today like Yogurtland.

My 90-year-old grandma (she never tells us her real age) is an immigrant from China. She came to America in the 1940s and worked until she was about 80. She was born in a generation where elbow grease and hard work was just how you did things to make a living and provide for the family. I vividly remember catching the bus from Chinatown in downtown San Francisco to travel the 45 minutes to SFO (which is actually 2 towns away near Millbrae). She would sit there on the bus with her purse tucked under her red sweater while she folded dollar bills into beautiful origami pieces of art. You might be asking yourself, what does this have to do with contact centers and customer service? This was in the late 1990s and there were next to no self-service kiosks, self-serve yogurt companies, and very little to no self-service contact center tools. This was a time where we waited in lines and depended on that 1 on 1 relationship with that hard-working grandmother behind the frozen yogurt counter to serve us.

What we didn't know at the time was that the world was about to change. As consumers we were somewhat complacent with waiting in line. We didn't want to do the actual work of pouring our own yogurt or checking out our own groceries. We actually cared to have that 2 minute experience with the customer service representative that was helping us. Giving us a glimpse into the life of the person behind the counter. In this case that old Chinese lady that had to ride the bus every day from Chinatown to serve us frozen yogurt. Giving us time in between putting in your order and paying, when you could ask her questions like; "did you make these dollar origami pieces?" and "is this your grandson helping you today?"

As you might have already guessed TCBY has gone the way of the dinosaur and has been replaced by these self-serve frozen yogurt shops. These have seemed to pop up on every street corner of towns, cities and even within the majority of our malls. You can even invest into these business at minimal cost or risk and get a sizable return on your investment as frozen yogurt is rather cheap to make. When using these self-serve machines, you aren't going to get that visually perfect swirl that you would get from someone like my grandma, but you do get to customize your cup by adding whatever flavors you want without regulation. As you make your way from the frozen yogurt machine over to the toppings station, you start to formulate how you are going to get the best (your favorite flavors) in every bite. No need to choose just one or two toppings, toss one piece of everything on there from chocolate to gummy bears. You pay by the weight, go to town!

This is the allure of self-service, getting what you want when you want it. It may not be the prettiest or highest of quality, but you get speed and customization. If you really want to take the time to make that swirl just right, then you have the choice to do so. This is what your customers want from your contact center. Don't force them to get the traditional support when you can let them self-serve and customize to their hearts content. This is where AI (Artificial Intelligence), Machine Learning and automation come into the equation.

Just like the self-service frozen yogurt stores, grocery stores with self-checkout, and banks with automated bank teller machines, you will find that self-service automation will require less staff and overhead. This is a true win/win for both customers and the company. What is the secret to achieving this self-service automation layer for your customer service? How can you get to the level of self-serving easy (level 1 and level 2) transactional inquiries into your Customer Support without sacrificing the Customer Experience?

To find the solution start by looking into your Customer Journey Map. Find out where the Customer is starting to have a poor experience. Refer back to the **People, Process, and Product** model mentioned in chapter 2. Take the time to survey your employees to collect feedback on; "what they think can improve the journey and experience". Look at your customer's responses from the CSAT surveys to see if there is some direct feedback about your **People, Process, and/or Product.** Another great tactic is to have a group of your decision makers and executives go to the contact center to shadow calls and experiences. We have done this with all of my past companies and it always provides amazing results.

About 8 years ago, at one of my previous companies, we shadowed calls and dug into CSAT surveys and found that the **People** on the team were performing at a high level. We also found that the **Processes** that we had in place (both internally and externally) for customer support was working really well. We found two different types of feedback that pointed to a much-needed **Product** (Technology) change. The first was there were too many nested options and menu prompts for the IVR.

The customers had to go through 3 to 4 different nested menus that eventually got them to the right team member. This was extremely frustrating for the customers that wanted do a simple transactional action like reset their password. The other issue that needed to be solved was that the customer had to mention their name and customer ID when an agent answered the call. This isn't that bad of a customer experience for most contact centers but was compounded when they had to spend multiple minutes going through menu prompts just to get to an agent. Causing the whole pre-agent experience to take upwards of 5 minutes before being put into the phone queue. This was not only an issue with my previous company, but also a hot topic for a couple of the companies I worked for later in my career.

Long IVR menus, having to repeat basic information and the lack of self-service for simple tasks are great indicators of the lack of the self-service automation layer of support. See chapter 1 for more detail around the *service onion*. After identifying the lack of **Product**, we decided to research how to solve this with technology enhancements. The first thing we focused on was to create an integration between our CRM and IVR/ACD. This was to help utilize *data dips* into our CRM when the person calls in. It helped identify who the caller is and if they were a special customer to us, so we could play specific messages and/or route them appropriately. We used this to help lower the number of options and menus in the IVR by removing the options that didn't have value to them. For example; we removed sales options to existing customers and removed support options to new potential customers. We identified customers who had a high likelihood of canceling and routed them to retention specialists instead of regular support agents. When we had issues that only affected specific customers we would play a unique message to them letting them know, without affecting the other customers experience. This was all designed to help speed up the process with routing and identifying customers pre-agent to help reduce costs and increase CSAT.

Another technology tool we implemented was an integration with a 3rd party to help completely remove the IVR and menu prompts. It uses Machine Learning and natural language AI to help route or solve simple issues. We branded this system AI Anna to give it a more human touch/feel. Instead of a traditional menu where it would ask, "Press 1 for..." it asks, "How may I help you today?" From there AI Anna identifies inquiries using predetermined AI call flows and routes the call to the appropriate queue. If it is a simple task it processes the task by using the same *data dips* as I mentioned before. I dig a little more into data dips and specifically how to use them in chapter 5. We used AI Anna to deflect calls and chats, decrease handle time and improve average speed of answer. After creating this technology for Phone (Virtual Agent) we decided to create a duplicate of the technology for Chat (Chatbot).

There are many partners out there that can help with this type of technology, we decided to go with one that would help us with the development of the tool(s). This is so we could focus on the call and chat flows that would dictate customer journey and experience, instead of having to develop the technology from the ground up. This allowed us to outsource the more complex development tasks/work so that we could have people internally that only focus on the experience and outcomes. If this is something that you will be implementing in the future I highly recommend finding a partner that fits your company's needs. As these 3rd party partners get more prevalent in the contact center technology space we will see more and more of the contact center world adopt self-service automation. Enabling us all to spend more time on perfecting the experience for the customers and conversations that are more valuable to have. Leaving the level 1 and/or transactional tasks to self-service automation. This is exactly like the self-service kiosks at airports, ATM machines at banks, self-checkout kiosks at grocery stores and self-serve machines at yogurt shops; but designed for the contact center.

It might seem that self-service is providing less of a white glove service, because it isn't 1 on 1 with someone via the phone, chat or email. It can actually be perceived as a very good experience and even preferred. Some customers will (and are already starting to) expect this as a service model, much like I expected this when I needed to contact my Airline for a refund of my double Wifi charge. This may be generational based off your customer base and type of service, but it also may span across all customer demographics. I recommend testing this as a proof of concept first with a small sample set of your customers before forcing this change on them.

Self-service automation is really leading the charge towards a **Frictionless Experience**. Much like the traditional effortless experience it will allow customers to handle issues on their own. It reduces the need to talk to a live agent and creates an experience that can truly be frictionless. Even in the best experiences with a live agent there are some potential areas for friction. Through things like; frustrating conversations, responses (or lack of), miss-communication, tone, pitch, etc. These aren't as prevalent with an AI bot or virtual voice agent. These human imperfections can be smoothed out by utilizing bots that proactively identify to the customer that they are not a human but can still solve issue for them. This will help the customer with mundane (easy) tasks that don't need human empathy or expertise.

After looking though some CSAT responses at one of my contact centers we saw a very strange pattern that was emerging with a specific agent. The agent was being too empathetic when trying to assist with some of these very mundane tasks. After pulling up some recorded QM calls we found out that the agent was saying "sorry" after hearing that the customer need their password reset.

The agent was saying "sorry" in their phone voice which came across as insincere. Customers were confused and commenting that the agent shouldn't be sorry and just needed them to perform the password reset task. By being over empathetic in these situations it actually made the customer feel like the agent was mocking them for forgetting their own password. Automating these types of tasks is not only more efficient for you and the customer, but it can prevent potential friction.

There is a common misconception that organizations should be using self-service automation only for transactional experiences. These are commonly FAQ bots and replacing IVR menus. AI and self-service can be so much more than just feeding your customers some static FAQ information while they wait for the next available agent. They can use *data dips* to pull dynamic content from community forums, take action on accounts, pull information from 3rd parties, and so much more. For one of my contact centers where there is a high volume of inquiries on shipping status we used a *data dip* into our CRM to pull shipping information to allow for customers to see where their packages are and what the carrier is. We would also use similar *data dips* to allow the customer to take action on their account, things like cancel membership or add a discount (used as a save offer) for customers who are frustrated with their service/membership. These types of self-service tools can solve real problems, instead of just regurgitating static information that can just be googled.

The key to success when trying to figure out what can be done for your unique customer base is to look at the Customer Journey. Map it out and take an outside-in approach to solving these self-service automation topics. Try to understand the customers' needs first, then try to solve for the issue type (or intent). I don't recommend starting by looking for calls and chats to deflect because you have high volume in a certain area. After understating this from the customer viewpoint use the *Golden Circle (invented by Simon Sinek)* to help plan for your next steps. Really look at **Why** customers are contacting you, then figure out **How** you can design a *frictionless experience*, and finally **What** you can create to support the inquiries. This method can help you really drive success with self-service automation. See *Figure 3.1* for the details on the Golden Circle.

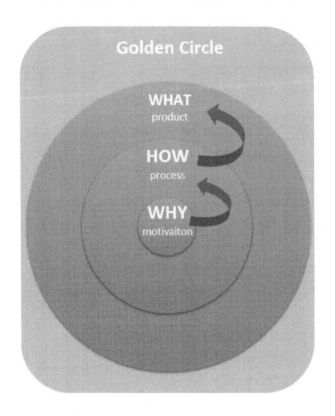

Figure 3.1 Golden Circle by Simon Sinek

AI is unique in that it is the learning mechanism that feeds back into itself over time to create better outcomes and experiences. It is the eyes, ears, and mouth of the digital technology landscape. This coupled with Machine Learning helps the AI be even more robust at making calculated decisions. AI is like the growing and learning toddler that needs a parent to help guide it to success. Machine Learning is the parent that gives the AI guidance as it develops over time. Without guidance from Machine Learning it can grow into an unwieldy tool that creates a poor customer experience. With these two tools carefully calibrated to work with each other, in specific areas of support, you have the ability to really drive marketing, user acquisition and customer engagement. These tools can be implemented over almost any service or sales channel and can be designed to keep, find new, re-engage, and even service customers. We are coming up on a technological age where *human like* interactions, that happen in our everyday life, will be carefully curated and crafted by AI and Machine learning bots. For example; a Facebook Messenger direct message can originate from an AI bot that knows exactly when the right time to engage you with a new product or opportunity. Learning from the product purchase history and your seasonal spending habits, it can send a direct message to you with a new replacement or upgraded product at a discount that fits your customer value to the selling company. This would be a rather simple AI Facebook Messenger bot with a Machine Learning algorithm that feeds in your unique customer data.

Another key tool for self-service is FAQ and Contact Us pages. Traditionally these are designed to help bridge the customer from self-help to traditional support channels like; phone, chat or email. With the invention of AI and Chabots, companies have embedded their proactive chat features on these pages (and other website pages) to help serve up self-service with an automated bot while they are consuming help FAQ content. There are some companies out there that have created an even more robust option for these pages. It is called the Self-Service Catalog and it is a tool that you implement on your FAQ/Contact Us page that allows customers to walk through workflows to complete simple tasks. It leverages the same API data dips that your Chatbots would consume (I go in greater detail on this topic in the next 2 chapters) but visualizes it through your support pages. These tools are designed to help you deflect easy (tier 1 type) questions like; password resets and order status. Just another way to leverage your existing technology to enable self-service.

4

Get off the Ground - Live in the Clouds

Over generations of evolution birds have adapted the ability to fly. This is an evolutionary trait that helped them from being vulnerable from predators and allowed them to be higher in the food chain due to their vertical advantage while hunting on prey. It also allowed their species to migrate to support the continuation of their species. Examples like weather and food scarcity are the common factors for birds to take to the skies to migrate. Oddly enough there are birds that used to be able to fly but have evolved to be flightless. This is/was due to the migrating species finding an environment (usually an island like New Zealand and the Galapagos) that doesn't have predators and has bountiful food abundantly accessible from the ground. Once humans colonized these remote islands and environments and accidentally brought over land-based predators into the remote ecosystem, these flightless birds started to go extinct. The most famous of these birds is the extinction of the dodo bird (chicken or turkey sized flightless bird). This was a flightless bird that was located in a tiny island off of Madagascar and became extinct when Dutch sailors landed on this island and started to hunt the dodo. It wasn't afraid of humans as it had been on this island without any predators for generations. Another key factor is that when the Dutch sailors landed they also brought pigs, dogs and rats (accidentally). All of these new animals enjoyed the taste of the dodo bird's eggs (which were in nests on the ground) and would often go hunting for them when uncaged.

Unlike the flightless birds like the dodo, most birds that aren't extinct today can fly. Some birds can fly within weeks of being hatched. The average bird learns to fly about 1 to 2 months after they hatch. There is an obvious advantage for them to have the ability to fly and do it quickly. This isn't much different for contact centers. Think of the natural predators as your competition. Your eggs or newly hatched birds are your technology tools. Using old technology and on-premise tools are like being flightless. Using cloud-based tools are similar to learning how to fly, giving you and your team the ability to be more agile and innovative to your business needs.

Today information is everywhere. Information lives in open databases and can be easily accessible via open APIs. For example; code to find out what city and state an IP address is from is accessible for free via API. Another example is using APIs for basic information like the distance between two addresses. All of these hard problems are now easily solved with open API in the cloud. With traditional on-premise tools it is hard to program in these basic inquiries without having to store data in a local server database. And even so, that data might become out of date or stale over time without regular updates. This is why it is ideal to get off the ground and soar with the eagles up in the clouds.

Open API isn't the only benefit to using this strategy. There are many others like; scalability (both cost and flexible capacity), reduced personal to maintain IT and NOC roles, ability to innovate easily, and many more. The biggest risk is with security and control over uptime. Even on-premise tools have a security and uptime risks, so this shouldn't cause too much concern for most businesses. If you have a highly regulated business (health or governmental industry) I would recommend scrutinizing these areas in the RFI process when you are looking to move to the cloud. Even with those risks I would highly recommend moving to the cloud if you haven't already.

Moving or having your technology stack living in the cloud also comes with the added cost of having to have people on staff who are skilled in improving and maintaining this new set of tools. This requires a different skillset of team members than the traditional on-premise IT support. Some products don't integrate easily with each other and that can create the need for project and product managers to launch successful initiatives. Another side benefit to working with vendors and partners in the cloud is that those products can be updated easily and effortlessly without having long downtime or internal resources to manage the changes. This can allow you and your team to work "on the business" instead of "in the business".

Similarly, another added benefit to cloud-based platforms is that they have pre-determined ecosystems that already easily integrate into each other. These come in the form of app store options (usually associated with a larger technology partner in the space) and widgets. These are usually out of the box solutions that can easily integrate two similar products together. A great example of this is the integration of a CRM and ACD/IVR. Something like Nice InContact and Salesforce Service Cloud. Integrations like these can be custom or they can come out of the box from one of the partners app store to create things like screen pops or easy *data dips* for caller identification. This is something that can quickly increase customer experience and lower cost of delivery by just enabling these features. Although some specific use cases might want to be customized, the out of the box solutions can usually get the job done without too much internal work. Trying to accomplish the same experience with on-premise solutions might be much more difficult to project manage and come at a higher cost.

What is preventing you from going to the cloud? Is it preference? Or just the way it's always been done? Or is it a security/control reason? Whatever the reason, I recommend reassessing and mapping out the reasons why you can and can't make the change. If the answer is "not right now" then try to reassess in another 6 months or a year. On-premise solutions are going extinct like the MP3 player, switchboards, MySpace, and the dodo. No innovative and adaptive company is investing as much time, energy, or money making sure that the on-premise solutions are current and up to date to beat cloud-based alternatives. They are just trying to maintain those products so that companies can utilize them until it is no longer valuable to upkeep the ongoing technical debt to keep these products afloat. Every major innovative contact center solution is focused on the development and progress in making the best Omni-solution cloud-based products. Which also comes with a high focus on global delivery and connectivity to broaden their products market. This is where individual cloud companies are spending the billions of their development budget year after year. It's best to jump on this bullet train as it is still gaining speed as opposed to trying to catch up once it has left the station.

Let's take a step back and think about the solutions that help a contact center operate. There are the core pieces; IVR/ACD, CRM, WFM, etc. Then there are the secondary parts; self-service tools, bots (chat, social, phone), in product help guides and tools, Customer Journey tools, speech analytics, etc. Let's not forget about measuring tools; data and KPI visualization tools, QA/QM and speech analytics, customer insight and CSAT, employee and company feedback tools, etc. All of these tools are vital parts of the big picture. If you don't have these in place you might not have the best experience or ability to measure the success of your department. It is easy to keep these silo'ed and report the opportunities/success of these separately, but if you don't integrate them it is hard to tell a true and full story. They often rely on each other to help us paint the full picture or customer journey. It's like painting a picture without having the ability to mix the colors. It still tells a story but doesn't allow you to paint a detailed picture that looks lifelike. In addition, these tools need to be able to integrate with each other and other external tools/data sources. For example, a CRM might need to connect to an ERP system (Enterprise Resource Planning) to help with purchases while engaging with a customer service agent. These tools are critical to a contact centers success as they allow them to process and resolve issues without having to transfer to someone else or process a request post conversation (open a ticket).

Implementing this ecosystem is easier than you would expect. Most vendors/partners out there today know that this is a requirement for doing business and will gladly start the conversation with what other cloud providers they integrate with. In fact, some companies are only built in these cloud/widget ecosystems and don't have a standalone product. A couple of examples of this are tools like; IVR voice translations and caller identification. These are products and vendors that don't sell as Omni-solutions, they rely on larger companies to integrate into so that they can optimize the solution to its highest potential. This is just one example of how cloud solutions can be pieced together to create a better customer experience.

Where should you start? There are some very important key decision points to consider when you are thinking of cloud solutions.

Easily integrates with other cloud-based technologies:

This is by far the most important decision point to make. The best benefit of cloud-based products is that they can work together, like a customized intra-net of products to be configured to work specifically for your business needs. Some vendors will say they are cloud but have limited API capabilities and/or can only integrate with specific cloud ecosystems. Some of the larger cloud providers (like Salesforce, Oracle and Zendesk) have widgets that are unique to their products. This can be beneficial and also a hindrance, depending on your unique business needs. Finding a partner that can work agnostically with any other cloud solution is a key differentiator in the market.

Scales easily up or down based off of business needs:

Products need to be able to grow and shrink with your business without high level of cost or complexity. Ideally you should pick a partner that can bill you accordingly monthly based off of usage, but if that isn't possible find a product that you can adjust licenses easily (or manually) so that your monthly or yearly bills don't get stuck at a higher peak rate. If there aren't scalable billing options I would recommend negotiating your contract to lower you price based off on what you think your baselines will be throughout the year. Scaling is also important from a staffing perspective. The worst thing that can happen for a contact center is having staff members hired but sitting idle because of having to wait for technology tools to be created or logins to be activated. Same when decommissioning licenses. You don't want to be caught paying for user licensing that is sitting idle as you ramp your staffing down. Having a good partner that won't hinder you in these areas when your business changes is key for any business. Cloud-based products usually have more flexibility and are more agile to support these changes in real time, vs. having to wait for a solution.

Connectivity and uptime service levels:

This is critical for any business and something not to forget about when considering cloud. Since these products are cloud and in a shared ecosystem, most large cloud vendors provide services that include very high service level and uptime. This is due to them having spent the developmental budget to be able to keep these very high service levels standards. When selecting a partner look at the past 3 to 5 years of uptime. This is usually provided in the RFI process or published online (especially if it is a public company). It usually comes in the form of a percentage like 99.9987%. This is commonly known as the four or five 9s (depending on the number of 9s there are in the Service Level until there is the first non-nine number). Ideally you want a company with at least a four 9s although three 9s is acceptable as well. Four 9s is an allowance of 52.5 minutes per year. Three 9s is an allowance of 8.7 hours a year of downtime.

Shared or dedicated environments:

This is dependent on your preference or needs. A shared environment will allow your provider to potentially better serve you by learning from other companies on your environments. It can also come at a lower overall cost. These are valuable when you have a Machine Learning tool that needs large amounts of traffic to perfect its confidence or success ratios. There are benefits to having a dedicated environment where your business can't be negatively affected by other companies on your cluster. Dedicated environments in the cloud might be slightly costlier but are valuable if you are a large organization that will use the mass majority of their clustered server services. When you are at a size/scale that is that large, it might be beneficial to move to a dedicated cluster. It is also important to inform your provider of seasonal spikes and forecasted volume. If you are a season shop that does the majority of your business around a holiday (like Black Friday) you want to make sure you are on a cluster with other customers who aren't spiking in volume at the same time. There are benefits to both, it is important to understand your requirements before you decide on what works best for your business needs.

Dedicated support and sales teams:

Another lesser known benefit to these types of tools is the ability to get included or premium support and sales packages. Some of the larger cloud partners assign dedicated support representatives and perform QBRs (Quarterly Business Reviews) that help you understand the benefit of the past service and leverage the partnership moving forward. Along with this dedicated support you can be a participant in a community with other similar customers that are experiencing and solving business needs/problems. Being a member of these customer communities can yield more than just support on common issues They can help you brainstorm new solutions for new initiatives or help you see how other businesses leverage their technology partners. Most of these are showcased through white papers, webinars and during partner conferences. When engaging with a cloud provider you also have the ability to potentially bundle services so that you can get a lower potential cost.

How do cloud environments work in the real world? It can be hard to see cloud-based ecosystems in action as a customer because the experience is so quick and frictionless. In reality, there are large workflows that are working in the background to make sure you don't feel any friction. Here is an example of a complex setup in the cloud that can help provide a better customer experience along with some backend automation. The figure below demonstrates multiple types of *data dips* (explained in more detail in the next chapter) into internal cloud tools along with open internet data. The *CRM* and *API Call to Open* boxes demonstrate the power of using the cloud to pull in data into a workflow for an IVR (for phone calls). See Figure 4.1 for an example of a workflow using *data dips* in the Cloud.

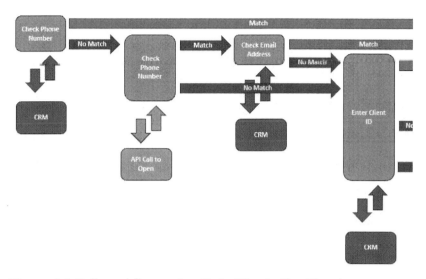

Figure 4.1 Call workflow using Data Dips in the Cloud

Starting a cloud-based project can be daunting and overwhelming. There are plenty of tools and technologies that help you solve or automate your processes. The key is to start simple and small. Try a proof of concept or A/B test first. Don't try to solve the complex problems right off the bat. Find a potential vendor to help you with an area of business and slowly roll out the change. A great example of this was when we decided to roll-out a Social Bot for Facebook Messenger. We started with a proactive notification that let them know where their package was post purchase, a simple shipping status notification system via Facebook Messenger. This helped deflect calls into our contact center and self-serviced our customers through a channel they preferred. After the proof of concept was successful we decided to add other functionality to the bot that allowed our customers to modify their membership and customer profile, through self-service. All of these enhancements helped with increasing self-service and customer satisfaction. The real success was the slow roll-out and measurement of each initiative as we grew this automated tool on Facebook Messenger. We could have deployed all of the different bots at the same time, but it would have taken us longer to project plan, develop and go live. If a cloud-based automation is one of your initiatives, you might want to phase the project out, so you don't catch yourself biting more off than you can chew in the beginning.

Another key topic when deciding to go cloud is to make sure your organization is technologically mature enough to handle the change. Some of the automations, *data dips*, KPIs that you will work with might need to be vetted appropriately by other department within your organization. If your internal business partners (or other departments) aren't prepared to partner with you on these cloud-based upgrades, it can set your development and deployment back. The obvious one to engage first is your IT security teams. They need to make sure you are using tools and partners that fall well within their security requirements. Make sure to get a NDA in place early when engaging with potential partners to move the process along. Other departments might need to be involved like; engineering, development, marketing, and accounting. We found that some of the customer service-based products we used actually had rich customer data that was beneficial to our marketing teams. This data can help with customer segmentation, cross and up-selling. You can leverage your cloud-based support channels to re-engage customers to purchase more products and/or share positive experiences to their friends and peers. If your internal business partners aren't technologically mature enough to handle this information, it could hinder the benefits you might gain from implementing these technologies.

One of the biggest benefits to cloud-based ecosystems is that they are easy to rip and replace if needed. You can piece together multiple tools/vendors as needed without heavy implementation or decommissioning time/money spent. This makes it uniquely appealing to companies that have to be agile or change often. A great positive example of this is contact centers that are setup as an emergency response to some sort of disaster. For example, governmental or non-profit organizations that need to stand-up thousands of contact center volunteers for events like hurricanes or hunger relief. This allows the organization to down scale and decommission tools as needed when the event is over.

A unique side effect of this is that it makes the competition between the competitors in this space hyper-focus on being the cheapest, best in class, and/or best to support. Since there is no long-term stickiness to these tools you can easily jump to another ecosystem or tool. The vendors/partners in this space are aware of this fact and use it to their advantage from a sales perspective. Since everything can be easily integrated, it allows these companies to quickly acquire each other to gain a better portfolio of products in their ecosystem. When this happens it not only allows the customer to negotiate a bundled lower rate and additional free services but can help cut down on integration times and costs. This is because the newly acquired companies are already highly compatible and have developed long term connectors between products. They eventually share similar or the same technical stack and/or infrastructure. Ultimately cutting down on any unique dependencies that you might have with multiple tools integrating to each other. As these larger cloud ecosystems get built out, they bring with them a level of uptime and security. As a consumer you start to gain some unintended benefits that might not be felt on a regular basis due to their size. See Figure 4.2 below for an example of a cloud ecosystem.

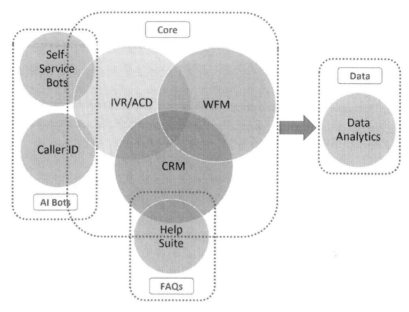

Figure 4.2 Cloud Ecosystem Example

If you are still grounded by on-premise systems, you might be feeling these pain points. It can feel like you have roots holding you down and preventing you from being able to change. Once you start to live in the clouds all of the roots fall off. You can be as agile as a hummingbird and move from flower to flower without much issue. Or in this example, product to product. This is not for every organization or business. If you have harsh governmental or regulatory rules that you must follow you might be more of a tree than a hummingbird. You might need to have on-premise solutions to keep you grounded and comply. As technology gets better the agile-ness of the cloud is getting more secure and bleeding into the governmental/regulatory compliance industry. They have already solved for most of the common compliance's like; GDPR, PCI, and HIPAA. But if you are unsure if they cover you and your business make sure to add that to your vendor selection process. Don't try to be nimble like a hummingbird if it doesn't make sense for your business.

5

Tortilla Chips and Data Dips - Smart Routing Techniques to Save any Party

There is nothing like going to a house party or BBQ and watching some major sporting event with friends. Something about hot sunny days with cold beers, friends talking trash and betting each other which team will win, score first, etc. buffet tables full of what seems to be an endless supply of BBQ hot dogs, burgers and chicken accompanied by chips and dips. My preference is to skip the BBQ and go straight for the chips and dip. Especially the home-made guacamole and 7 layer bean dips. I'm a sucker for both of these when I go to a summer BBQ. The worst is when one of those coveted dips runs out! Much like these coveted chips and dips, there are similar technology techniques that can really save the party. This is where *data dips* come into play.

You may be asking; what does this have to do with the contact center? Just like how a chip plunges into that salsa or guacamole and quickly exits to get consumed, you can program technology to do something similar. Using an IVR (the chip) to dip into a Database (like a bowl of guacamole) to pull out the exact information you want. This is how *data dips* work. They are quick small API calls into data warehouses to quarry points of information to help the IVR decide on the next part of the flow. An example of this would be; John Doe calling in to chase bank to check his balance. The IVR would ask him, what is your bank number? After getting the information it would use an API call to find out his profile information and ask him to verify some other information; like email address or zip code. Once John was authenticated it would do another API call to find out his balance and repeat it back to him over the phone, eliminating the need to transfer to a live agent. Much like eating a chip without dipping it into guacamole can be similar to sending the customer to a live agent without doing any API *data dips*. If you want to lower costs and increase customer satisfaction I recommend using *data dips* and automating this process. Or in this example, dipping the chip into guacamole... it just tastes better.

How does this apply to the contact center? How can this technique save my company time and money?

Agents usually have to take call after call (or chat or email) and often times they have to do the repetitive mundane work of asking the customer to verify their account or have the customer repeat something they already answered previously in the IVR. Or even worse, the agent has to tell the customer to hold while they look up their account. These are all poor customer experiences that we can avoid. *Data dips* are how companies can provide secret superb service without customers even knowing. Using this methodology can help in multiple different areas. They can support simple requests automatically or even start a process (like collecting information for a case/ticket) so the Agent can get to the meat of the issue.

Data dips fall into three categories; **Authentication**, **Transactional**, and **Proactive**. See Figure 5.1 for each of the three Data Dip Categories.

Figure 5.1 Data Dip Categories

Authentication data dips are exactly what it sounds like. It is the tool that searches your CRM or some public internet record to push some basic customer information back into the IVR. This can be used to verify someone of a customer or member status, verify they have paid their current bill, or even search for secondary verification records (like email or street address). Although this data dip doesn't really take any action, it can be a very powerful way to; be in compliance, proactively automate an action agent would normally do, or help verify basic profile information like phone or email address. The most common automatic single verification method for this is searching for the customer record within a CRM database based off of ANI (customers phone number). It is always a surprise and delight scenario when you call into a company, who you normally do business with, and it greets you by name. "Thanks, Aarde for calling AAA Insurance, how may I help you?" This is just a simple way to start the conversation off on the right foot.

Transactional *data dips* can help take action while in the IVR (pre-agent). These can be things like performing password resets, updating profile information, writing cases/tickets for agents to review later, etc. Depending on the complexity of your requests it can do actions like; insert payment information to update a credit card on file or order food from a restaurant. All of these are possible with proper tooling and *data dips*. These techniques are helpful for call/chat deflection, which will reduce volume into the contact center and reduce overall costs. These tools can really automate level 1 requests. These can be the best cost savers of the contact center as they directly affect the volume coming into the support organization.

Proactive *data dips* are more for agent efficiency. These are things like; CRM screen pops, triggering emails to customers after the call, asking them if they would like the call to be recorded and/or if they want to fill out a survey after the call. A great example of a proactive *data dip* is to initiate a proactive notification when something changes for the customer in the future. This can prevent the customer from wondering what happened and needing to call in and cause unneeded volume into the contact center. We use Facebook Messenger as a proactive tool to send our Members a notification letting them know that their product has shipped. This has proven to reduce confusion and increase customer sentiment. One of the tools that is the biggest game changer, with proactive *data dips,* is CRM screen pops. This is becoming standard for most contact centers and a key tool to reduce AHT (Average Handle Time) and increase Customer Experience. These prevent the agent from having to lookup a profile when someone calls in. The case, ticket or profile automatically pops up when the agent answers the call. The IVR takes the phone number associated with the caller and looks up the customers profile. Once it gets the customers unique profile number it can send it to the agent when they answer the call. This is all done in the background, so the Agent doesn't have to verify anything with the customer over the phone when they get connected. All of these techniques can help lower agent talk or handle time and reduce overall costs through efficiency. See Figure 5.2 for an example of a CRM Screen Pop workflow.

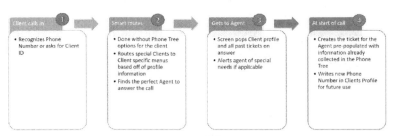

Figure 5.2 CRM Screen Pop Workflow

All of these can be coupled with AI third party tools to leverage natural language responses instead of forcing your customers to go through complex numbered menu prompts. Remember the goal here to create a *frictionless experience*. The more friction the more frustration from the customer as they go through these workflows. Although you don't need to have all products/tools in the cloud to achieve these *data dip* connections, it is easier when you have cloud-based tools that support open API. When searching for potential products/partners you should make sure they have adequate documentation on their open APIs. The important API connections should have the ability to **GET**, **POST** and **PUT**. With those three methods you should be able to accomplish the majority of the 3 types of *data dips* I highlighted previously. See below for a quick definition of each method.

GET is used to request data from a specified resource.

POST is used to send data to a server to create/update a resource.

PUT is used to send data to a server to create/update a resource.

The best thing about these is that you don't have to roll them all out at once. You should take your time to prioritize these projects based off of potential implementation time/effort, costs, ROI and non-financial ROI. I recommend doing some resource planning, so you have dedicated team members assigned as responsible for these projects. For larger organizations (or companies interested in investing heavily in this area) I would recommend hiring a Project Manager to help organize and support these initiatives. We use tools like the **RASCI** Model to help assign the appropriate stakeholders to the projects. See Figure 5.3 for an example of the **RASCI** Model.

R - Responsible - who is responsible for carrying out the entrusted task.

A - Accountable (also Approver) - who is responsible for the task(s) and who is responsible for the project as a whole.

S - Support - who provides support during the implementation of the activity/process/service.

C - Consulted - who can provide valuable advice or consultation for the task.

I - Informed - who should be informed about the project progress or the decisions in the individual tasks.

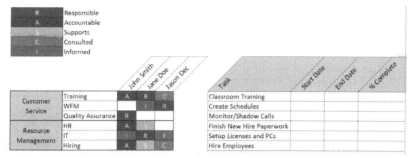

Figure 5.3 RASCI Model Example

With the **RASCI** Model you can help allocate resources, so you can manage multiple of these projects at once. It might be strategic to have one set of team members working on **Authentication** *data dips* while another group of team members can work on **Transactional** *data dips*. You can have some of these projects run in parallel so that you can have a sooner go live date for all of them. While the **RASCI** Model can help you with identifying who or what teams should be working on what projects, it won't tell you which project has the highest priority.

To help with priority setting we leverage the **Priority Pyramid** methodology to help us understand what projects to work on first. This prevents us from getting distracted with the less valuable projects at the bottom of the pyramid or back of the backlog. See Figure 5.4 for an example of the **Priority Pyramid** Methodology.

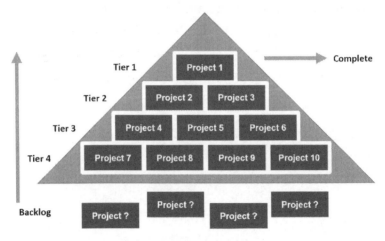

Figure 5.4 Priority Pyramid Methodology

The team works and focuses on the top priorities first (Tier 1) then works down to the lower tiers. It doesn't mean that we only focus on the top projects first before starting the others. It just means that, if there is a set amount of resources and time constraints, that the team should focus on using the resources on the higher priority projects first. It is important to move projects to the top of the priority based off of financial ROI and non-financial ROI metrics. Examples of financial ROIs can be things like; reduce Cost of Delivery (COD), lower recurring variable or fixed costs, increase retention and customer saves, and increase sales or customer Lifetime Value (LTV). Examples of non-financial ROI would be things like; increase Net Promoter Score (NPS), increase Customer Satisfaction (CSat), increase Customer Experience Score, and reduce Customer Friction/Effort.

Although all of these metrics are important, it is important to create a Customer Service Mission and Vision Statement first. If you have a very clear Mission or Vision, it can help with the prioritization of these pyramid projects.

When we really start to work on these projects we leverage tools like the **KIT (Key Initiative Tracking) Summary Board**. This a tool to help break down these projects into segments and track the completion percentage for each of these Key Initiatives. We can use a colored circle to indicate a(n); on track, at risk, critical or not started status. This, combined with a RASCI model can help us find the blockers (or critically at risk) parts of a project and who is Responsible and Accountable for the completion of them. See Figure 5.5 for the KIT Summary Board Template.

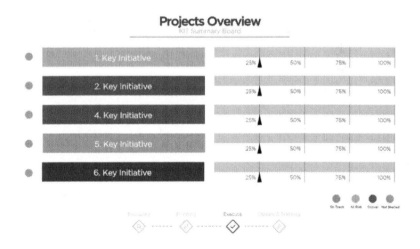

Figure 5.5 Key Initiative Tracking Board Template

With the right tools, methodology and people in place these key initiatives can be accomplished rather easily. Don't forget to focus on the customer experience when designing these changes. Everything should be driven by customer experience and creating a *frictionless experience*. Some of these projects can seem daunting, but I recommend taking your time in the planning phase, as it will help you out long term. Alan Turing, the father of theoretical computer science around the concepts of algorithm and computation Artificial Intelligence, once said; "Those who can imagine anything, can create the impossible." This is especially true when it comes to projects, of any size, that can help change the customer experience. You often have to imagine a new experience for your customers before you can create them in real life. Integrating your core systems so that they talk to each other is key to the success of your contact center.

As I mentioned in chapter 1, *Bullseye routing* can be an amazing strategy for improving not only customer satisfaction but potentially decreasing handle time. There is a strategy out there that couples the idea of *Bullseye routing* and persona-based routing, I will touch on this a little later in chapter 11. This is a concept that segments your customers based off of a persona profile and pairs them to the team member who is the fastest at potentially answering that customers inquiries. Persona Based Routing is highly dependent on *data dips* and integrations into your (and external) databases.

I consider these techniques as the framework that will help you succeed with a lot of the other ideas within this book. These are like the tortilla chips and dips that will save your tailgate or house party. Like any party, you still need the key items in place (BBQ hot dogs, burgers and chicken) before you focus on the "nice to have" features you want to implement (chips and dips). Some of the key tools are; IVR, ACD, WFM, CRM and QA. Those are the core of your technology stack where everything else might be add-ons to one or all of those tools.

6

Pick a Partner not a Vending Machine

Why do people still like to go to restaurants when you can have food delivered right to your door? What about going to a store and buying something vs. just ordering it online. There are plenty of examples of how we can be consumers and never have to speak to a real person. My favorite one is the Vending Machine. These are the boxy refrigerator sized machines that have spiral horizontal metal hooks. They rotate to deliver you a bag of chips or candy bars once you add money and press some combination of letters and numbers, like A6. These are inventions of an earlier era, designed to easier self-service customers in areas where you couldn't staff a general store or snack bar. Reducing the cost restraints of paying someone to stand behind a snack bar 24/7 in areas like hospitals where there is limited space to setup a physical shop. Although vending machines are a great example of self-service automation in a physical world to select a product, they are not great for complex product purchases. Buying a candy bar doesn't require a sales person to help with the decision process but imagine buying a more complex product like a house, car or boat. For these more complex and costly products it might be more beneficial to work with a sales representative before you decide to buy it.

When you are going through your vendor selection process, think of new technology products like a true potential partner to your business. You should ask them questions that have to do with your business needs (both now and future) as opposed to just buying a "thing" or "product" to solve your issue(s). The new product can help enable your business and it can be a functional technology to help with complex workflows and tasks, but your relationship with these vendors goes much further than that. You should engage them from a consultative perspective and have regular meetings and QBRs (Quarterly Business Reviews) to help support your business goals. Although they are not direct employees of your company, it is important to highlight to your service representatives that they are an extension of your team. At my current and past companies, we would often lean on them for escalating issues or new feature requests on our behalf. Holding them accountable for key performance metrics, and/or involving us in development release notes and kickoff meetings. This is much more than just purchasing a product, we are building a partnership with these technology vendors.

Why do we still crave that human interaction? For some instances self-service is not ideal. Simple transactional conversations or tasks can be done using self-service (like vending machines and ATM cash withdraws). For those times where you know a long-term relationship is required, it is better to continue with good old fashion face to face communication. Think of it like dating; you wouldn't buy something from a vending machine for your meal on your first date. Or order something to go or delivered to your door. Ideally you would take, or meet, your date at a restaurant for a sit-down meal to build that face to face relationship. This is why most sales representative like to take you out for happy hour drinks or a lunch. Why do we do this? It's to show the level of commitment and how much you value that potential relationship. You want to do the same with your partners. You don't need to take them to a dinner (although breaking bread can often help), but meeting with them in the beginning and setting expectations can go a long way towards building a healthy partnership.

Another area to focus on is your potential partner's maturity. Not necessarily emotional maturity (although that is helpful too), but how mature they are from a technology standpoint compared to your needs and others in the market. You don't want a partner that is always trying to catch up with you and your requests because they are not equipped to handle your businesses size and complexity. You also don't want a partner that is much more mature than your business and normally deals with larger/more complex business. This usually leads them to trying to sell you on other add-one or products that may be too complex or not needed with your scale or immediate business needs. These relationships can become toxic and you both will always be expecting more from each other instead of being content with the relationship. See figure 6.1 for an example of how to choose a partner and not a vendor.

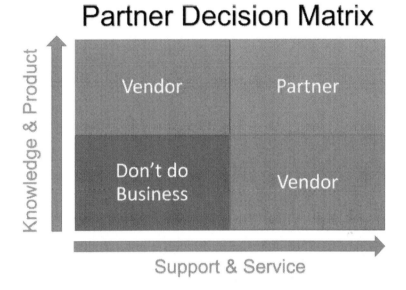

Figure 6.1 Partner Decision Matrix

When using this matrix try to rate your potential partner on a sliding scale of 1 – 10 for each category. The upper right would be the 10 out of 10 for both categories while the lower left is 1 out of 10 for both. This will put them into a quadrant that dictates if they are a good partner or just a vendor. If you want help with a more detailed selection process, try doing the same thing for the following areas below.

This is different for each company, and often can be referred to as an RFI (Request For Information) or RFP (Request For Proposal). I recommend making a short list of your own businesses requirements and assessing some potential partners that may fit first before going too far in the procurement process. Here is a short list of areas where you can rate a potential partner from 1 - 10. You can use this on current partners to assess if you have already selected the right partner.

Technical Maturity:

This is a great metric to measure if a company is ready and able to do business with a company of your size and complexity. Sometimes your partner might be more mature than your company which is not desired. While others might not be mature enough. You wouldn't want to buy a race car to go grocery shopping in every day. You also don't want to use a skateboard. It is important to write your company's technological requirements in a list format first, so you have a checklist to work from when you are asking potential partners their technical maturity.

Support Acumen:

They not only can support your business from an uptime and service standpoint but can also "speak your language" when resolving or releasing new features. These interactions should be timely and communicated in a way where both parties fully understand. This is where healthy debate and conflict can be leveraged to build a stronger relationship. Regular meetings and business reviews are good to keep the conversation going so one side of the partnership doesn't "suffer in silence." This is one of the most important criteria as poor or nonexistent communication can be toxic for any relationship.

Basic Business Fit (company location, size, and sustainability):

If you have highly important requirements in this area it is important to stress it. If you are global you shouldn't find a partner that can only service a specific region. Be aware of the partner's company size. You may need to lean on multiple people from a specific department and if they have a team of less than 5 in that area it can be challenging. You should be cautious of partnering with a company that is too big, as this can cause "passing of the buck" with your issues and they might become lost in the vast sea of other client's requests. I recommend researching the company's financials (if publicly available or shared openly). Be cautious if you are their largest customer or one of their first 50 customers. You might enjoy the additional attention in this scenario but be cautious of the company being bought out or dissolving in the near future. You should always work with a potential long-term partner for larger, critical technologies.

Product Features:

This is a very important requirement. Make sure they fulfill a full match of your "need to haves" vs. your "nice to haves". The nice features might lure you in, but if there are some key product features missing it is best to pass and look for another partner. Although technology product features shouldn't be the only key factor to picking a partner, it is an extremely valuable cornerstone in your long-term success with this partner. I don't recommend banking on your partner telling you that they will develop these product features for you in the future and add them to an upcoming release. Assess the product as it is today, not what it can provide you in the future.

Additional Value Add:

This is where you can leverage your new partners for QBRs, customer communities, educational conferences, white-papers, webinars, customer references from other similar businesses, etc. Although this isn't as valuable as some of the other requirements I listed above, it can help you keep the relationship healthy long term and create some additional value add.

Sometimes the process of picking a potential

partner can take weeks, months or even years. It is important to let your new potential partner's team know where you are in the process and let them know what you are expecting from a timeline perspective. You might have an eager sales representative who is looking to close a deal by end of quarter. If this is the case, make sure to not rush into the decision making process and wait until you and your business is ready. For some of these larger (foundational tools) I recommend putting a timeline together and having phases to this process. I use these project timelines for larger product tools like; CRM, IVR/ACD, WFM, and Social Moderation. Some of the other smaller 3rd party tools don't need this robust timeline as they can be selected and implemented much quicker without all of the necessary steps. Here is an example of the phases and tasks that I try to map out. See figure 6.2 for an example of a complex partner selection timeline.

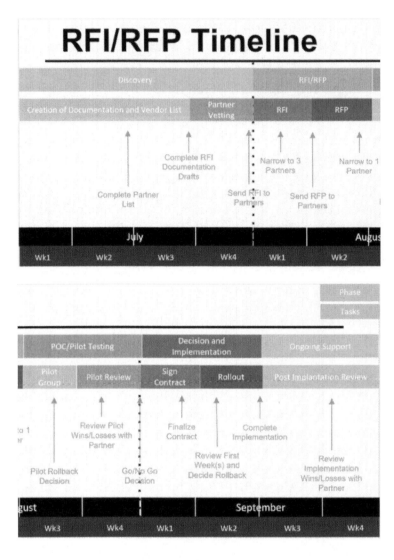

Figure 6.2 Partner Selection Timeline

1. Discovery Phase

This is a time for you to vet all potential partners

and gather your internal business requirements. Sometimes this is the longest phase, especially if you don't have a dedicated project leader and/or you need to gather requirements from other key internal stakeholders. Good rule of thumb here is to make a matrix or list of potential partners and don't start eliminating. Allow all potential partners to be eligible in the beginning. This list can be rather long to begin with but will quickly be reduced once you get to the next phase(s). You can utilize online product review tools to help collect some basic information in your matrix as needed. Some good ones are Capterra and G2 Crowd. These are the Glassdoor like websites for technology products. If you are attending conferences, make sure to do some online research first before getting bombarded at a Demo Hall by sales representatives. The conference Demo Halls can be overwhelming and unproductive if not researched ahead of time. Think of this phase as the being single but putting yourself out there and exploring potential relationship options.

2. RFI/RFP Phase

During this phase you will send each of your potential partners a list of questions that pertain to your requirements and business needs. It is always important to get a NDA (Nondisclosure

Agreement) in place between companies during this phase so you are both protected if any private or proprietary information is shared either way. Make sure to initiate this with an assigned sales representative and try not to communicate with more than one representative at a time. This will save you time and confusion later in the process. Don't be quick to asking for pricing, which can come later, as pricing is negotiable and sometimes you can always lobby internally for more funding or a better deal with the partner. As a best practice, you might want to put together a short summary of your company, department and partnership expectations/goals. Remember that this is a two-way partnership and they will need/want to know more about your business and objectives. This phase can be short (if you're lucky) or can sometimes loop if you find out negative information that can eliminate potential partners late in this phase. As you potentially go into a proof of concept (POC) or pilot phase you might want to discuss the potential of having a limited contract for the first couple of months. This is to eliminate as much commitment risk on your side if the partnership doesn't work out. Remember that good partners don't necessarily mean that they come at a high cost. In fact, as some partners become larger and develop a best in breed product, they start to gain economies of scale. This means that they can provide higher and better services for a much lower cost to the customer. Think of this phase as the dating time-frame of the relationship. You use this time to get to know each other before you commit to anything.

3. POC/Pilot Testing Phase

Proof of concept and pilot testing is crucial to the success of any large technology launch. This is where you can A/B test with small groups of agents or push your new product into production by starting at a small scale. Usually this is a 1 - 2 month process where the product is checked for its compatibility in a live production environment and validated by the business. It's important that both the business and partner are highly engaged during this phase. There should be daily/weekly feedback and KPI sessions to track the success or failure of this test. This usually ends in a "go/no go" meeting and hopefully leads into a full product roll-out. If a contract was not fully negotiated and signed at the end of the RFI/RFP phase, it is important to get one in place before moving to the Decision and Implementation phase. Think of this phase as the moving in or getting a pet together phase of a relationship. You can really get to see if this partner is going to be the right fit without committing or risking too much.

4. Decision and Implementation Phase

For larger tools it is valuable to present the results of all three previous phases to a steering committee or executive level team to get buy in and guidance. Don't forget to include a portfolio of the potential partner and try to outline what the future of the partnership would look like. If you have a proactive partner, they will help with the content for this phase. This is also a time to transition from the sales side to the support side of the relationship with the partner. You will want to start engaging with the support organization of this partner to see if they are a good fit going forward. It is important to identify who and how to report and potential ongoing issues and identify any rapid response items that will need to be resolved ASAP. Think of this as the introducing to parents and getting engaged phase. This is where you want to show your level of commitment and gauge if the other person is as engaged and aligned in the long-term success.

5. Ongoing Support

Always remember that the support process never ends. Even the healthiest of partnerships should be reviewed regularly to make sure the partnership is in alignment. Your partner should be there to support you in your business changes and growth. I also recommend going through the first two phases (Discovery and RFI/RFP) every couple of years as you or your partners and businesses might change. This can be a signal to the current partner that you aren't satisfied, so be cautious when contemplating this strategy. Some partners will be open to hearing about you starting a new RFI/RFP and it will trigger them to rebuild the relationship. This is very similar to telling your significant other that you aren't happy with the relationship. You can imagine how some partners would react to that news.

There is a time and place for choosing vendors vs. partners. These are usually for tools that don't necessitate a heavy support relationship and/or implantation. A great example of this is Microsoft Office. There isn't a need to pilot or support overly complex use cases. You just purchase licenses and deploy as needed. These are turn-key products. Another example of a vendor like product that I have used for multiple deployments is a tool that improves caller identification. These are tools that add on to the IVR and use API to ping, with a **GET** API call, public records to help identify a phone number to known email addresses and names. Much like Microsoft Office, this tool doesn't need strong partnerships with a company and only requires a vendor to provide the API technology.

If you already have large core products today and aren't leveraging your partner to its fullest I would recommend revisiting that with them and calling out what you expect moving forward. Some larger technology companies have tried to monetize these relationship models into tiers like; premium or platinum support. If you are a valuable customer of theirs you can always negotiate these support price points down to fit your budget. Even if the price is too high you can ask for additional addons that make it more valuable (like onsite visits) to add to your customized support package. The best way to ask for these benefits is by having an open conversation with your partner and highlighting your company's worth/value to them.

When you are looking at cloud products it is important to know the four main ways they usually charge for these services. The four main pricing models are;

1. **Concurrent Peak Licenses** - Highest utilized licenses at the same time within a period (usually a month). This is usually the best pricing if you have variable volume.
2. **Named License** - Max used licenses used in a period (usually a month). This is usually at a slightly discounted price to offset idol licenses throughout the month.
3. **Volume Usage** - Price per transaction or conversation during a period (usually a month). This can also be structured by time (usually

minutes). This is best for scenarios where you can throttle your volume up or down as needed to hit budget constraints. This is an ideal pricing model if you need control over volume and spend.

4. **Permission Based Licenses** - Price per tool-set usage volume over a period (usually a month). This is helpful if you have tiered users of a product; super users, admin, front line agents, light agents. Ideal for negotiating on discounting due to the lack of a full product feature set.

When vetting out a potential partner you want to make sure you have the right key evaluation points to help you make your decision. Here are some that might help with this process;

- Platform and product stability
- Ease of use and training
- Ease of implementation
- Reporting and analytics capabilities
- Agility to customize or integrate
- Usability for team members and admins
- Platform and product roadmap
- Omni channel and omni solution-based product portfolio

Now that you have the criteria to potentially select a vendor, what are the next steps? It is important to gain buy in from key decision makers internally early on, so they aren't blindsided by any new/large requests. Remember to plan out potential internal resourcing (headcount needed) to support the initial implementation and ongoing maintenance of the product(s). Secure a budget from your finance team that allows for some buffer, in case there are unexpected costs or delays in launch. Try putting together a proof of concept (POC) at little to no cost to prove out the potential partner and tool-set. Try to negotiate an opt out clause in the contract so you have the ability to roll back or turn off this new tool without financial recourse. This is usually done to prevent as much risk to the company as possible.

With all of these best practices in your back pocket you should be better equipped to find the best potential partner. Much like choosing a car, house or even significant other, remember not to rush and to do your due diligence. Just like Goldilocks you want to choose a partner that is "just right" for every business need.

7

The Best Defense is a Good Offense - More than a Cost Center

Whether you watch sports or not you can recognize that sports are not only an important part of modern day culture, but also a key part of human culture and evolution. Ever since the first game was invented it was used to pass the time and distinguish a clear winner and loser. They played these games on boards in Russia, in the form of chess, and on fields of modern day Mexico where the Aztecs played Ullamaliztli, which is an ancient ball game similar to a combination of Soccer and Basketball. These games combine strategy, skill and endurance and eventually would be the backbone of worldwide competitions like the Summer and Winter Olympics, and World Cup of Soccer. Most of these games are won by focusing on a very strong offense or defense. While defense in important, you usually can't win with only defense. Points are usually derived by some sort of offensive drive/action. While there are some games that allow you to score while on defense, it is more likely that the offense drives the points on the leader board.

Much like sports and board games, business has clear winners and losers. Not only with competitors in the same space, but individual moments in sales and customer service as you win or lose business. Sales and marketing usually have clear win percentages for campaigns while customer service has customer loyalty and retention campaigns that record wins and losses. Any business can be defined by these KPIs and the individual internal departments own these specific areas of business. Most commonly sales and marketing own acquisition and incoming income/gross margins (your offensive team). Customer service usually represents service delivery and retention (your defensive team). While both are important, it is important to master your team's objectives first before exploring ways to potentially blend these teams.

As a result of this you may notice that the majority of the budget and funding usually go to the offensive teams and new customer acquisition. Often times customer service teams are pressured to be more cost effective and/or drive down costs. This is where the term "Cost Center" has come to be used. It is used to describe a negative cost instead of a positive savings. The question is; how can you turn the negative perception of your contact center being a "Cost Center" into a revenue driving positive "Profit Center"? It isn't easy, but it can be done. Perception is everything and tracking KPIs to prove this change is critical to your success. It is important to start with and maintain a healthy strategy for turning your contact center into a revenue protecting or generating machine.

This is like a football's defensive team getting a

safety or intercepting a pass and running it for a touchdown. Or a hockey team wasting time with the puck in the final seconds of the game while they are leading in goals. These are examples of when a defensive team can help you win the game. This is similar to a customer service team up/cross-selling and retaining customers. Both of these are ways to prove that your customer service contact centers are increasing and retaining revenue. In rare cases goalies (defensive players) in soccer and hockey have been known to make goals in the opposing teams nets, by kicking or hitting the ball/puck across the full length of the field. This is just another example of the defense turning themselves into an offense player that can change the outcome of the game. This example is like turning a detractor into a promoter after an amazing customer experience. Another great defensive strategy in football, basketball, soccer, hockey, and other field games; is to keep your opponent in the opposite side of the field so it makes it more difficult for them to score. This allows you to control the time clock, so you can waste time while you are ahead in the overall score. In the customer service world, you can do something similar by creating great self-service options, so your customers don't have to contact you. That is like the 50-yard line barrier in football - between self-service deflection and contacting you via traditional channels. Great customer self-service is the first layer of defense for your contact center. Design and utilize it to help keep the customers happy and run down the clock (extending their Lifetime Value).

Like I mentioned earlier, you don't want to focus on changing your customer service contact center until you have stabilized your service and customer experience. Working on turning your center into a revenue generating profit center isn't a priority until you solve for any other issue you may have. Make sure your CSAT, NPS, and CX is hitting your goals before starting any new initiatives. Some of these value-added strategies may improve these customer service metrics, but the goal of these strategies is to increase value to your company through a traditional customer service lens.

Before we get into value added strategies, let's talk about customer LTV (Lifetime Value). LTV does a lot more than just retain your customers, it brings in recurring or projected new revenue. Protecting your LTV can help with customer retention, loyalty, satisfaction, experience, and increase word of mouth through Net Promoter Scores (NPS). LTV is (Total Revenue - Customer Acquisition Costs - Customer Retention Costs). See figure 7.1 for an example of the Customer LTV formula.

Figure 7.1 Customer LTV formula

Traditionally the focus for a customer service department is to reduce customer retention costs, but things have changed with the advancement of technology and Omni-channel support. Now that customers can contact you across any channel they prefer, for anything they would like, customer service teams have to adapt to the change. Customers want to be able to get customer service and support while also potentially buying something new or upgrading their membership. We are no longer in the age where it is ok for a customer service representative to put the customer on hold while they find a sales representative to transfer them too. With the right value add strategy you can start to create an increase in your company's total revenue while still servicing your customers. Not only will this increase your value to the company but help you to lobby for more budget and funding as you go to the table during your company's budget forecasting time.

Tony Hsieh, previous CEO of Zappos once said; "Customer service shouldn't just be a department, it should be the entire company." What he means is that every person in the company is performing some level of customer service. We shouldn't forget to appreciate the team members that do some of the harder customer service jobs every day. Jobs like de-escalating aggravated customers and mundane jobs like password resets. Honoring those employees and moments with your customers is where the real value add is for your company.

Here are a couple of value add customer service tips that can help you turn your contact center into a profit generating team.

Create brand awareness within your contact center:

This is key when you are working with internal or external (outsourced) contact center representatives. Hire team members who live and breathe your brands. Create days and events around your company's brand. If it is a consumable product, give your employees the product as a reward for being loyal. This will help them understand what the product is and what being a customer feels like. If you sell a physical product, convert an area on the contact center floor where the agents can go in and physically feel and interact with your brand. Another good idea is to put up banners and visual areas that foster the brand colors, logos, mission, and vision. If your product is a service, you can also gift your employees the service. I once worked at a health and wellness software company where the employees got to spend $50 worth of credits on a service or gym of their choice.

Direct sales, cross-sell and up-sell with agents:

Enable and empower your customer service agents to sell your products and services. Whether this is physical product, service, or an add-on to an existing product. This shouldn't be required, but agents should be empowered to do this as needed. You can run gamification campaigns to reward and incentivize this behavior daily, weekly, and monthly. This is often naturally accelerated if you already have a great brand presence in your contact center. We have heard our team members say things like; "I use this for the gym down the street and it works perfectly." If you really want to leverage this, I recommend having a gamification tool to track sales KPIs and drive agents to sell more based off of certifications/badges. Creating a commission structure around this also can have a positive return on the investment.

Direct sales, cross-sell and up-sell with an IVR while customers wait:

Another area where you can sell is in your IVR. You could inform your customers about your new products, promotions, features, etc. while they wait for support. It's important to be cautious about selling too aggressively via your IVR, but don't ignore the power of selling while waiting. Supermarkets do this all of the time, think about all of the products in the checkout line like; gum, magazine, candy, etc. It is important to have a *data dip* technology in place to complete this sale through the IVR without having to send this over to a physical agent. Suggestive marketing of your services and products while customers wait is a potential way to increase brand awareness and potentially increase customer longevity, Net Promoter Score (NPS) and Lifetime Value LTV.

Smart routing potential sales to best support agents:

This can be a little complex and advanced to setup, but once it is done correctly it can really increase your ability to convert or close sales in your support contact center. The idea is to use Machine Learning or a simple customer value score to help route more valuable (from a sales perspective) customers to agents that are more proficient at converting them. If you share your CRM with your sales team and they already track this customer value score, you can easily leverage it to bullseye route to agents who have a higher conversion rate. This can be a complex Machine Learning algorithm that feeds into a complex *Bullseye routing* system or it can be as simple as routing your promoters (customer who are loyal) to high performing agents (maybe your Tier 2 Support). With a little bit of strategy and training you can really increase sales and turn your team into a profit center.

Create tiered support packages for the opportunity to up-sell support:

This strategy doesn't work for all support centers, but it can work for some. This is more valuable if you have complex support, long wait times, and/or a customer demand for dedicated support. You can create support packages for purchase that give your customers things like; dedicated representatives, accelerated case resolution, accelerated priority in queue, expanded support hours, and/or access to executives or other internal teams. This is a way for your support team to create a revenue generating program that can prove the customer support team's value to the company. If you want to try this, I would suggest creating 3 different packages that customers can choose from. Something like; bronze, silver, and gold. When there are 3 options the customer usually chooses the middle or top option. This approach can set you and your program up for success, driving them to packages that can better benefit both the customer and the company. It is important to create a contract (or contract amendment) to help support this change, this prevents any risk if someone purchases one of these packages. It is important to track this over time to make sure you are providing the promised services to the customer, so they feel that the add on service has met their expectations.

Involve support teams in sales and marketing team meetings and kickoffs:

It is really important to cascade information from one department to another. If done properly, this can break down silos and reduce improper sales when done by a support representative. You don't want your customer service team selling an old package or product. I don't recommend spending too much time into training, as this isn't the primary role of the support representative. If possible, try to focus only on training the team on what they need to up-sell as needed. When you have a blended support and sales team you can even leverage support team members to help with sales if sales start to slow down. Allowing for a cross departmental alignment can help the company as a whole. This is another important potential value add to the company.

Deliver KPIs so that they drive results:

Reporting the KPIs of this program can sometimes be tricky. If the right story isn't told it can result in mixed messages to the agents and others within the company. If your team is primarily a support team with a little bit of sales blended in, you should reflect that in your agent/team KPIs. You don't want these agent-facing reports to drive too much competition and gamification around the sales aspect if it isn't where their focus should be. This can be done by visually removing the sales KPIs from regular reports. Example; if your support to sales goals are 90%/10%, report on support KPIs to the team weekly and sales related KPIs bi-monthly (or monthly). The way you communicate this information will drive behavior and performance. Be sure the messaging and timing reflect the overarching team and company goals.

Time the sales pitch so it works naturally in the conversation:

If your team has more of a scripted support response make sure that the up-sell isn't an afterthought. It is better positioned naturally into the conversation, if possible. By putting it at the end of the conversation it can come off as off-putting to the customer.

Successful sales conversions usually happen when the conversation is structured like one of the following;

Sales -> Support

Example; "Before I help you with

that, did you know we have a product that supports you in that area?"

Support -> Sales -> Support

Example; "As we continue talking about your issue, did you hear about our support product/tool that can also help you?"

They often don't work when structured this way;

Support -> Sales.

Example; "Before you go, have you heard about this product that we have?"

This is because the connection between the customer and agent has already come to a close and the sale (after support) can feel cold and not welcomed. It is equivalent to trying to catch someone with a sale as they are walking out of your physical store and have their back turned to you. You want to engage with the sell while the conversation is warm and still inviting.

Something to keep in mind is that customer service teams are perfectly fine being cost centers. It's ok if you have a team that is positioned to only be defensive. Most companies do this by design because it has proven to work. If it isn't broke, then don't fix it. Companies want their best team members protecting their recurring revenue or customer base. Most major companies became successful based off of their customer service reputation. This is the core of the fabric that makes up customer service. For some companies this is less black and white. Sales and service can sometimes be blended and go hand in hand. It just feels natural based off of the customer group and product offering. Depending on your company's environment a solid strategy for either can accelerate your department's success.

Remember that not all of your customer service team members can be equipped to sell. You might want to create varying levels of blended agents to support with this blended model transition. Sales can come naturally to some while others might have a more difficult time transitioning. Proper training applied to the less naturally talented team members is a great way to round out the team. A good routing strategy can help validate if the conversation or customer type that is calling in has a higher chance of buying something and route appropriately to a team that is blended with this sales skill set.

Even with something like a 10% uplift in revenue can really prove the value in key initiatives like this. Potentially turning the perception of your cost center into something positive for the greater organization. How can you leverage your traditionally considered defensive team members into a game changing offensive force? I recommend inviting the sales team leadership early into the strategizing part of this planning process. They should be key stakeholders in any transition into this blended model.

When you use these techniques you not only can help with LTV, but you can also start to brand your contact center as a profit generating team. It is very important to continuously think about the customer experience when designing and implementing these value-add programs. You don't want to fully turn your support team into a sales team. You may not want to infuse sales into the support team if it doesn't make sense either. The goal is to break down barriers and allow selling when appropriate. This strategy isn't for all customer service centers, I don't recommend trying to force it to work in an already productive support driven environment. In the game of business, it is often important to utilize your players to their fullest potential. Remember that defensive players can also be very good at offense (when needed).

8

LLTV - Key to Long-lasting Life Time Value

Long-lasting Lifetime Value (LLTV) is something that is hard to achieve. To succeed you need to create an overall experience through every customer touch-point to create raving fans of your brand. There are some key areas to help this become successful for your business, but they aren't easy. Chris Grosser (a famous photographer for ESPN, Sports Illustrated and the New York Times) once said, "Opportunities don't happen. You create them." This is true with most things, but even more true when talking about customer satisfaction and lifetime value.

Customers want you to; "Value me, know me, hear me." In this day and age, customers know you have data about them and want you to not only know their value, but also know who they are. There is a fine line between knowing too much about your customer and knowing just enough to design a meaningful experience. You want to leverage just enough information to not be creepy. For example; I wouldn't want a pizza place to know where I lived if I never gave them that information ahead of time. Unfortunately, that basic information is already out there and can be leveraged to create faster conversations if desired. I do want them to know my address and name based off of my phone number if I have already used them in the past. This would speed up the ordering and payment process, so I don't have to repeat myself every time I call in.

Another important strategy for any customer service team is to focus on NPS (Net Promoter Score). This can be done by protecting recurring revenue or creating a longer lasting positive experience when the customer contacts you. Net promoter is rooted in how likely the customer will recommend your brand/company/product to someone else. Other than calculating a LTV value like I mentioned in chapter 7 (refer back to figure 7.1), how should you think about increasing this value? How do you increase this score and experience by leveraging an offensive strategy with a traditionally defensive team?

Jeff Bezos (founder and owner of Amazon) once said, "A brand for a company is like a reputation for a person. You earn reputation by trying to do hard things well." We can all learn from Amazon and how they have become the marquee example of a company with exceptional branding and customer service. They took a long time (decades) to get there, but now that they are there, they are reinventing how customer success should be.

Here are some strategies that can help do hard things well;

Use positive language in every form of

communication:

Think about how you position your brand and company. From the language you use on your website to your customer service agents communicating via; phone, chat, email and social. I recommend taking every written word and rewriting it so that it reflects a positive tone. Here are some examples;

1. Change "how may I help you?" to "how may I best serve you?"
2. "Contact us when it is most convenient for you: 24/7/365."
3. "Our team members would love to chat with you, click here to start a chat."
4. "Sometimes waiting can be a drag, we hope you enjoy this soothing music while you wait."
5. "Continuously improving is one of our key goals, please help hit this goal by proving feedback through a quick survey after your call."

Positivity in these messages can change a not so pleasant message into a positive one. Remember that if you promise something you have to deliver, you don't want to write or say something and let your customer down.

Customer Secret Service:

Leverage information you already know about them to provide a better experience. You may already have some data on your customers that can help segment them into a specific type of customer. Doing simple 'surprise and delight' actions can really wow your customers and keep them coming back. Here are some examples;

1. Give your highest value customer(s) priority routing.
2. Give customers who contacted you twice in one day priority routing, because they are probably calling back because something wasn't resolved the first time.
3. If your customer had a great experience with an agent before, route them to that agent again (if available).
4. Empower agents to give out free services or products once a month.
5. Empower agents to write hand written letters/postcards to valued customers.

Data driven smart routing:

Data can pay an important part in customer experience. Especially if you already know something about the customer trying to contact you. There is direct data (basic profile information), indirect data (contact or purchase history) and big data (aggregated scores and values based off of multiple data points). There are open source data options that you can either pay for or get for free via open API. Some companies have created whole business models off of providing proprietary data to you if you want even more insight into who is contacting you. Here are some ideas about how to leverage data to create better experiences;

1. Route based off of customer tier or value.
2. Route based off of customer geo-location or country (ANI or IP Address).
3. Route based off of previous experiences (called in the last 24 hours, bad previous CSAT score)
4. Route based off of past purchase history.
5. Route based off of customer profile or persona.
6. Offer special offers or deals to customers based off of customer data.
7. Deliver special messages to customers during peak volume times.

Go off script:

Empower your team to throwaway the scripts. Customers don't want to hear templated responses, they want genuine responses to their questions and inquiries. Scripts can create more "cookie cutter" quality experiences and it can come across as robotic and un-empathetic. You can deliver quicker more efficient conversations without using scripts and by training the team on direct communication techniques. This might take a little more skill and expertise, possibly come at a higher cost, but the impact on LTV is worth it. If you have an agent who is an expert at this, I would pair your new hires with them, so they can learn how to work off script more easily. I have found that people that work in fast paced face to face customer service environments are naturally the best at this. These are baristas who come from Coffee shops and waiters/waitresses from mom and pop restaurants.

The Double Platinum Rule:

The Golden Rule states, "Treat others the way **YOU** would want to be treated." If you want to be treated nice, you should mirror that and treat others nicely. The Platinum Rule is, "Treat others the way **THEY** want to be treated." This is an even better concept because you treat customers the way they would like to be treated, catering to their needs. The only issue with the Platinum Rule is that it may turn your team into martyrs. They might go to the extreme to support your customers without thinking about themselves or the company. I have seen team members stay late to resolve a customer's issue when they could have transferred the call to another team member. The Double Platinum Rule is slightly different, it goes like this, "Treat others the way **THEY** don't even know **THEY** want to be treated."

This concept can be a little harder to grasp. Here is an example; if someone calls in and complains about not receiving a package in the mail. Instead of reshipping the package to the same address (Platinum Rule), double check the address with the customer and adjust it to the correct address and then ship it (Double Platinum Rule). This might seem like the obvious solution, but for some agents they might just stop and reship the same product to the wrong address again, causing another call and loss money. This takes a little more effort into understanding what the root of the question or issue is. Preventing future frustration, confusion and loss of potential revenue.

Try to remove the word "no":

If you were to close your eyes and imagine the best place in the world, you most likely would think of a place where they removed all of the negative words like "no". A place with unlimited time, money, family, and happiness. It was Walt Disney's dream to create such a place. Walt Disney once said, "You can dream, create, design, and build the most wonderful place in the world … but it requires people to make the dream a reality." How do they do it? How do they have parks full of people and cast members (customer service team members) and remove the word "no" from the vocabulary? They start by training team members to answer hard questions with alternatives instead of "no's". Take for example an area that is designated for the parade and not available for people to sit or stand in. They usually rope this area off and have a team member stand nearby to answer any questions. If someone asks, "can my family stand in that roped off area?" Instead of, "no, I'm sorry it is reserved." They answer with something like, "This area is reserved for the parade, how about I help you find another area for your family to stand." The "no" is implied but never said, leaving room for the customer to feel like they never got shut down or rejected. Instead the customer feels like the cast member is helping assist them in finding a potential solution to their need(s).

Create career paths for your team:

Often times a customer service job can become boring or mundane. Doing the same repetitive task for 40 hours a week can get repetitive. For some contact centers the agent can repeat the same phrase over 10 times an hour. That is 80 times a day, 400 times a week. Imagine having the same conversation with someone 400 times a week. Without some sort of break that job can quickly become disenchanting. Not only is it repetitive and mundane, but it can prevent an agent from reaching the full potential that they have. If you infuse some new, on the job, learning in the equation you not only get diversified team members, you will find that they are more engaged in their work. Creating strong career paths and extracurricular learning programs will help with employee satisfaction and overall buy in. Google had a 10% program that empowered their team members to use 10% of their work week on anything they want. This not only allowed them to have time to expand their expertise, it also enabled them to do more than just the mundane repetitive work every week. We created a similar campaign at one of our contact centers and it helped agents learn about a similar topics or roles that they were interested in. We created direct career paths that allowed them to learn about complementary positions and roles in their field, within and external to the company. This program, coupled with the ability to choose their potential career path, drastically increased their engagement into their current role and company as a whole. It helped other departments with overflowing workload and allowed them to more easily recruit new team members from within, instead of having to look externally. Internal applicants had a much higher chance of gaining roles as they were already leagues ahead of external candidates not enrolled in the program(s). This increased the talent pool of qualified applicants applying into the contact center, as they all knew it was an opportunity to expand into a greater role at some point in the future. Giving employees reasons to be happy in their jobs leads to better one-off experiences for your customers that eventually drives to higher LTV and CSAT.

Pay employees based off of performance:

I will go over this in much more detail later in chapter 14, but the concept is rather basic. Pay your employees based off of their performance instead of tenure. Sometimes tenure and performance can be correlated, but often times for a more repetitive task, someone can achieve a high level of mastery in their job at a sooner time-frame (2 to 6 months). What you should be doing is giving a small pay increase after this on-boarding period to highlight their initial progression and then pay based off of performance on an annual basis. Performance in the contact center (specifically customer service) can be hard to track. I have found a very simple formula that can help with this and talk about it later in detail. You can weigh one metric over another, but it all boils down to "how well someone can do a task" plus "how fast/timely they can do that task." Once you figure out the magic formula of how to measure and track this you can create benchmarks and pay scales to promote productivity improvement. Some of your agents will be good at one area of the equation while barely passing in another. While some other employees will excel at both. The goal is to compensate your team based off of these KPIs to drive the overall team performance. When we implemented this in one of the contact centers, we had some front-line agents making more than their team leaders. At first, we were concerned, but soon found out that it was actually a good thing. It incentivized high performing agents to stay in their current role as opposed to incentivizing them to leave their role and become a team leader (which might not be their strong suits) just to make more compensation. When you focus on rewarding high performing agents you will get better quality as a team which is the backbone to LTV. I will go over this in more detail in chapter 14 including specific examples.

Reward customers as much as you reward employees:

Most customer service contact centers have a program in place that rewards employees. This is usually in the form of lunches, yearly parties, holiday time off, fun activities while at work, etc. Most companies forget to create a rewards program for their customers. All companies and brands are different. It is important to think of customer rewards that would work the best within your environment. Here are some ideas on how to implement this idea;

1. Incentivize customers to use self-service with rewards. Things like community engagement and FAQ creation.
2. Reward customer for not contacting you too often. You can give credits or perks to the customers who are the most self-reliant.
3. Reward customers for bringing major issues to your attention. This can help your QA, Development, Marketing and Sales teams.
4. Highlight your customers in testimonials. You want your best customers to get recognition and want other customers to see an example of a marquee customer.
5. Allow customers to beta test for you. This enables them to gain the benefits of being an early adopter while allowing you to gather preliminary feedback on product.
6. Reward customers with regional communities and education. If you have a complex product or offering, have traveling roadshows or webinars that enable customers to share regional or specific problems.

Don't speak in localisms or slang:

Make sure your agents aren't using terms that are only used in your local area, region or area. These are terms like "y'all" and "cool". Have them refrain from slang terms that may be not be popular or widely used. Especially slang that can be perceived as too cutting edge for a support team. Only use these if they directly represent your brand. An example would be a surfboard company using Californian slang like; "hella", "cool" and "rad". Another example would be a horse saddle company using "y'all".

Fill idol time with proactive communication and work:

Instead of placing a customer on hold while you wait for something to be processed, fill that time with something productive. Sometimes agents have to process a credit card or wait for a manager to approve something. While they are waiting for that action to be completed they can ask/validate with the customer their profile information. This can fill in the idol silence and help time pass by without the feeling of being put on hold. Here is an example of how this can work.

> Agent - "While we wait for your credit card to be processed, let me ask you a few questions to make sure your profile with us is up to date. Is your email... Is your address... Your monthly plan is... etc."

How Disney leverages LLTV to create lifelong raving Fans:

A great case study for a company that has really embodied these strategies is Disney. What really makes Disney locations the happiest places on earth? Is it the churros you get on the streets of Disneyland or Disneyworld? Is it the warm and fuzzy feeling when you walk through the gates and see Cinderella's castle for the first time? Is it the nostalgia that you feel when you see the familiar images and characters of your childhood come to life right before your eyes? Or is it the amazing secret customer service that you receive without even noticing it? I would argue that it is the latter.

How do they do it? What makes their customer service exceptional? I would like to start by saying that they aren't perfect, but they do some key things that makes them better than their competition. Remember that they don't have to be good in this area, they could have chosen to deliver the same product (parks, childhood nostalgia, etc.) without having exceptional service. They could have decided to just create a theme park and decided to not try to surprise and delight. Here is where they have decided to focus their energy to create long lasting raving fans of their brand.

Clean parks and brand image:

If you have been to a park it is clear to see that there aren't trashcans overflowing and utility workers (garbage men, bathroom attendants) just standing around or in plain view of guests as they roam the park. This was designed by Walt himself by use of hidden corridors behind attractions and buildings to keep this out of sight. Like an orchestrated play there are choreographed times where employees go on specific routes to pick up and clean out trash receptacles. He hired Industrial Engineers to time exactly how long it should take for garbage receptacles to get 75% full before needing to be changed. The trash bins themselves are placed no more than 50 ft from each other to prevent guests from littering. All of this was strategically planned out to prevent ruining the perception of a dirty park. Which in turn helps preserve your childhood fantasy that we all envision when growing up with Disney movies and shows. At Disney every cast member, regardless of title, has it in their job description to pick up every piece of trash they see as they walk around the park. It is even in the CEOs job description. Imagine how disappointed you would be if you went to Disneyland only to see your childhood fantasies ruined by trash littered everywhere.

Hire friendly staff:

Not every interaction at Disney is a pleasant one, there are outliers. For the majority of the time

Disney strives to make sure your interaction with their cast members (what they call their staff) is a great one. How do they do this? They train cast members to pay attention to the guest's requests. A guest might be saying one thing, but in reality, wanting something else. It's the cast members job to ask probing questions to get to the root of the request and help fulfill it, if possible. The devil is in the details. This translates to contact center service representatives too. Make sure your team is asking for the root inquiry and try to solve for that, instead of solving surface level issues. Disney does this really well because they ask probing questions in a friendly manner verses asking repetitive questions that can be annoying to the guest. Tone of voice is an important tool to use when trying to support a guest that might be agitated or dissatisfied. It's not only being friendly, it is making every guest feel important. Making every guest feel important doesn't necessarily mean that the customer is always right. Disney trains on being *assertively friendly*. This action is designed to actively seek out guests to help. Don't let a guest come to you. Instead, train your staff to notice an opportunity to service someone and proactively go to them and ask if they need help. This is an amazing way to enhance your brand as the customer already feels like you are there for their best interest. It positions you on the same side as the customer instead of the traditional customer => business relationship.

Create WOW moments:

Little wow moments can go a long way. For our company we use the term Surprise and Delight. An example of a company that has had success with this is Zappos (online ecommerce shoe/retail company). Zappos gives their employees a monthly budget (something like $50) to spend on their customers that they interact with on a regular basis. They do things like send customers little gifts when their product is delayed or didn't arrive on time. Disney is also really great at this. If a ride breaks down and you were in line, they give you a Fast Pass to another ride of your choosing. This Fast Pass allows you to skip the line on the next ride. They also have little perks like giving pins and badges to guests for celebrating milestones; birthdays, first visits, anniversaries, etc. These are all little moment of wow that bring joy to guests. Even if you don't receive any of these little perks, it is nice to see others around you receiving this level of service which turns it into an infectious positive environment.

Build relationships with guest:

A strong key to customer loyalty is making sure you turn transactional interactions into relationships. If you have ever been to a Disney park you might notice that there are kids (and adults alike) standing in line to take pictures with Disney characters. What you might not notice is that not only can you take a picture, but you can ask for a signature from the cast member. It might seem like a simple interaction, but this is a way to build a relationship with the guest. The reason those lines are so long is because a cast member takes every guest interaction and turns it into a scenario where the customer will feel valued. This means that the conversation or interaction can take a while and shouldn't be rushed. This is where you turn a customer's perception from feeling *processed* to feeling *valued*. Treat your customers like people and not like a source of income. This might not necessarily translate to your particular contact center, but it is something to keep in mind when you're thinking about extending your LLTV of your customers.

Be show ready:

At Disney they do training around being *show* ready. This means as soon as you are clocked in and at work you should be working as if you are center stage. Taking the time to prepare to become show ready is baked into their daily schedule. This means that uniforms and presentation are an important part of the job. This doesn't mean that looks are everything, it just means that if you are ready to help any guest or customer you should be ready to give it your best. Even the cast members dressed as Disney characters have to learn their characters unique signature, so that they don't break the fantasy. This is a great technique to train your team members on so when they jump on that first phone, chat or email they are on their A game and not dreading that first interaction.

Over communicate often:

At Disney they train their cast members on over communication and to do it often. Everything in a Disney park is scheduled and has been planned to be efficient. What happens when something is late or not going to plan? Disney will attempt to overcommunicate. If a train or ride is running late, a cast member will come on the loud speaker and explain exactly why the train or ride is delayed and how long it will be. We often forget to do the simple task of communicating to our customers when we know something might not be on time or delivered the way it originally was designed to be delivered. By just proactively over communicating (and doing it often) you can really increase the credibility of your brand/company. In the call center world, we have opportunities to do this all of the time. When there are outages, product issues, etc. we should use those opportunities to proactively overcommunicate.

If you are interested in learning more about Disney's story, I highly recommend reading Dennis Snow's (Former Disney employee for 20 years), "Lessons from the Mouse - Applying Disney World's Secrets of Success to Your Organization, Your Career, and Your Life."

With these techniques and strategies, you can change the perception of your customer service contact center into one that is much more positive. The goal is to allow customers to feel valued and heard. Ultimately, they just want you to; "Value me, know me, hear me." If you do it correctly they will turn into Long-lasting Lifetime Valuable Customers.

9

Creating a Frictionless Experience - Key to Customer Effort

Creating an effortless experience is something that is extremely important for any contact center. Effortless experiences can be described as experiences that don't cause large amounts of; effort, time, mundane work, and/or discomfort for the customer. Forcing your customers to choose a contact channel they don't prefer (like phone) or forcing them to fill out lengthy forms to open cases, are great examples of high effort customer service experiences. Reducing these pain points and increasing self-service capabilities can help lower overall customer effort and help increase Customer Satisfaction and NPS.

Customer friction is the phrase that defines the specific details that can lead to high effort. Creating a *frictionless experience* is something that can really take your customer service contact center to the next level. What is the difference between a frictionless and effortless experience. Effort is the force needed to overcome friction. Friction is the amount of force you create to prevent progress. I know this is starting to sound like a high school physics class, but it helps articulate how to think about customer effort. Think about a train that has to get from point A to point B. If it is a normal track it needs to use a normal amount of fuel and power to get to point B. Now if you had the ability to grease or ice the track, it would take less fuel and power to get to point B. This would be an example of removing the friction. You can design the experiences that your customers have. You have the power to reduce the friction on the track and grease the wheels. If done improperly you can accidentally line the track with tar and create more friction.

Instead of focusing on reducing effort, try reducing friction. A good way of identifying experiences with too much friction is by asking your customers what they don't like about the service experience. Another way is to have people go through the customer service experiences and track every detail about what was hard during the process. You can use secret shoppers or even task new team members to go through the experience before they start doing their normal job. Once you identified where you can improve, you can really start greasing the wheels.

When making business decisions make sure to be more than customer-centric, try to be customer obsessed. This will help you focus on how to create a support organization where customers are at the center. A good team exercise to see if your coworkers think with a customer-centric mindset is to do the capital E test. Grab some post-it notes and pens. Have your team put a post-it note on their head. Then ask them to write a capital E on the post-it note. If they write it so that others can read it then they are customer-centric thinkers. If they write it where they can read it in the mirror, then they don't have as much of a customer-centric mindset. Some people naturally have a mindset where they think of others first. These are the people you want to engage with when coming up with a customer obsessed strategy.

Here are some examples of experiences with friction that can be avoided.

Forcing customers to use lengthy support channels to do simple tasks.

"Be where your customers are." Don't force customer to move to you. Imagine you want to reset your password or need to update/change your address on file. If there wasn't a way to do this online or via self-service you might opt to try to do this via a chat channel. Some customer service organizations still force you to call in (and potentially wait in a queue) to do these simple transactional tasks. Identify these points of friction and try to change them to save your customers time and frustration. Allowing your customers to choose the channel of their preference is key to lowering customer effort.

Long and lengthy phone menus and prompts.

Imagine calling into and getting a main menu that has 6 options. Then once you choose one it goes to another menu with 5 more options. Then after that a couple of more options. Some IVRs have so many options and nested menus that it starts to become frustrating. If you have an operator (press 0) option, they will most likely just choose that instead of going through all of the menus. An easy solution to this is to try combining options, "for billing or support press 1." Another option is to look into AI virtual agents that utilize natural language to route calls. A good rule of thumb is to have less than 4 options per menu and less than 2 nested menus. You can try helping customers through these complex menus by having the selections in your contact us page(s) before it displays a phone number to call. You can even have a phone number dedicated to each specific queue, that are displayed in the contact us page after the customer selects what type of issue they have. The key here is to keep it simple. If you make it too complex you will lose customers to just pressing 0 or hanging up.

Limited or full visibility into wait times.

There are three types of ways to inform customers of their potential wait times for live queues (phone or chat). No visibility, which means that you don't inform them of any wait time. Limited visibility, which is when you let them know an average or longest wait time as an estimate. Full visibility is where you tell them exactly what number they are in queue and a time estimate based off of longest wait. With full visibility it can continue to remind them about their spot in line as they move up in queue and/or loop the message every minute. I have seen some companies display these times on their contact us page, so customers can decide if the wait time is tolerable to their preference before calling in. There are pros and cons to every model, it really depends on your specific company's preference and how long/large your queues normally are. Something to note about full visibility is that it can sway the arrival of your contacts based off of your customers preference. Customers might not call in if they know it is long wait. They might just wait until it is less of a wait or a slower time. This can make your contact peak and valley intervals smooth out over the day. This is both good and bad. Good because it can allow you to better staff for your average contact volume times and bad because your customer doesn't get service when they originally wanted it.

Annoying hold music.

Nothing's worse than waiting on hold or in a queue and getting really horrible hold music. The royalty free elevator music that everyone has grown accustomed to and associating it with calling a call center doesn't cut it anymore. This is often the first thing your customers hear when interacting with your company. Some customers may have to endure this song for more than 10 minutes!!! Not only is it an auditory pain, but it often loops the same song every 30 seconds. Yikes! No matter if it is your favorite song in the world, no one enjoys hearing it on loop every 30 seconds. If you run a report on percentage of customers that abandon after X amount of time you might be surprised that your abandonment rate actually increases right when these songs loop. When a song loops, it starts over, and the customer subconsciously thinks they are put to the back of the line (where they started from) and decides to give up/abandon. Perception is everything when someone is waiting in a queue. This can be a huge friction point for customers and they may not even realize it. There are 3rd party companies out there that help mix up the hold music options and some even allow your customers to choose their music genre. Just like giving them a personal radio station to listen too while they wait. Another strategy is to break up the experience by playing prompts (try not to be to sales focused) while they wait. I have even heard of a contact center playing a joke of the day for customers to lighten the mood. Another solution is to give them the option to wait in silence. Don't let them suffer through another minute of repetitive mundane elevator music.

Lengthy forms and ticket fields.

If you do require case creation and submission for support, at least try to cut down on manual and inefficient fields. If you can pre-populate data for them (maybe because they are already logged in) or create templated options, it could reduce friction when having to do this lengthy process. Removing required fields that aren't really required can help too. Some companies have designed UI/UX changes to help make this submission process for customers less painful. Moving all required fields to the top and making non-required fields less prominent on the screen is a great example of this. Another alternative is to embed self-help content from your help suite or FAQ pages while they are typing out their case. Instead of sending an email as a confirmation that you received their request, you can create a popup to notify them it was successfully submitted. Helping cut down on the number of emails you send to the customer. The ideal experience for the customer is having a customer facing dashboard that shows all open and resolved cases to help reduce confusion and duplicate submissions.

Repeating basic information over and over.

If you already have caller ID in place and agents are getting a customer profile information screen when answering a call or chat, then there isn't a reason to re-validate the customer when they call in. Instead of starting the call with, "Thank you for calling ABC company, who may I ask is calling?" It should be something like this, "Thank you for calling John, how may I help you today?" Something else usually overlooked is the experience when a customer needs to be transferred. If you have already validated the customers identity, then make sure to pass that information on to the next agent so they can start with solving the issue rather than wasting time to authenticate the caller again. It should go something like this; "Hi John, my name is Steve. I see you have been working with Jason, he filled me in on the basic information. Let's see how I can help you..." The last thing a customer wants to do is repeat their name and why they are calling over and over. If you create a process or use technology to help pass information from one team to another you will prevent a lot of frustration and friction.

Transferring to another department.

Customers don't want to hear; "I'm sorry I can't help you with that. You have to talk to ABC department for that issue." If you have the ability to cross train your employees (at least with basic information) you should. Another solution is to make the menu prompts very clear in your IVR, so customers don't choose incorrectly and get sent to the wrong department. You can even use terms and phrases that the customer would understand while in the IVR. For example: instead of; "For sales press 1. For support press 2." You should say; "If you are interested in buying something press 1. If you need help with a previously purchased item press 2." These minor changes can really help direct customers to the correct agents and prevent the need for transfers. If possible, share training content and international help suites with your teams so they can answer easy cross departmental questions.

Depending on your business, you might need to do some things to comply with regulations, laws, etc. Some of these can cause experiences with higher amounts of friction. Features like two-way authentication that are required for some protected customer information can be a time consuming and frustrating experience. I recommend taking a look into why these are requirements and choosing the best experience to cause the least amount of friction. If two-way authentication is required, try to make it easy with leveraging a connected SMS or email tools.

Focus on the flow of the customer experience. Really try to grease the wheels. Think about the individual pain points that your customers have and try to remove them. You can do this by shadowing support teams or use the feedback that you receive directly from your customers. It may be important to provide this collected feedback to other internal teams to help make changes. A modern example of this is the new Amazon Go grocery shopping stores. They are testing these in Seattle for Amazon employees. It is a grocery store where you literally just walk out of the store with your items(s) in a shopping cart and it will build a digital cart and charge your account. This removes the friction of the checkout process for groceries, causing one less potential friction point that can cause frustration. They designed these grocery stores after collecting feedback from customers about how the check-out process took too long. This is truly a frictionless experience.

Imagine a future where every potential friction point was removed. Imagine from the time you wake up till the time you go to bed, not having to do anything complex or mundane. No more resetting passwords, or even having to think about passwords in the first place. No more having to contact anyone for support or having to take out a credit card to pay for lunch or dinner. Or even having to carry things like wallets or keys. This futuristic utopian world may sound amazing, but we need to make sure we are automating the right types of tasks and interactions. The right ones are the transactional interactions (password resets, entering PIN numbers, paying for something at checkout). We don't want to automate everything because some interactions are better with a live human. Example of these are ordering food/drinks to a personalized preference and/or ordering a specific coffee at your favorite coffee shop. These interactions can be linked to nostalgia and selective preference, where longer more meaningful interactions are preferred. Even though this interaction can be automated, it feels better when done with a live human.

No matter where the world is going, we all know that technology and innovation will help us drive down friction. It is a competitive landscape out there and as the customer service industry evolves your competitors will evolve with it. It's important for you to be ahead of the adoption curve when it comes to *frictionless experiences*. The Everett Rogers Technology Adoption Curve (below), is a great visualization of when the market adopts new methodologies like this. If you adopt in the first 3 phases you are ahead of the curve and aren't lagging behind your competitors. See figure 9.1 for the Everett Roger's Technology Adoption Curve.

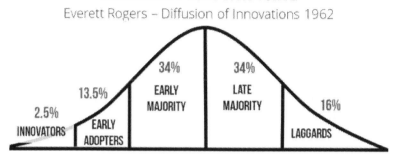

TECHNOLOGY ADOPTION CURVE
Everett Rogers – Diffusion of Innovations 1962

2.5%
INNOVATORS

13.5%
EARLY
ADOPTERS

34%
EARLY
MAJORITY

34%
LATE
MAJORITY

16%
LAGGARDS

Figure 9.1 Everett Roger's Technology Adoption Curve

As mentioned in the book *The Effortless Experience* by Matthew Dixon, Nick Toman and Rick Delisi; "What if the holy grail of service isn't customer delight but customer relief-the simple relaxing of the shoulders that comes from having your problem handled quickly and smoothly." Relief is that feeling of reduced friction. How can you help provide relief? Why not pivot from a goal of customer delight to customer relief? Are you measuring the success of your customer delight as a result of painful experiences that you can avoid? These are all very important questions to answer as you think through your current, and future support environment.

I don't want to downplay customer delight. This is very important for customer loyalty and should still be a KPI of your contact centers ability to deliver service. It's just important to measure this when you already have started to master a lower level of friction for your customers. By all means, focus on surprise and delight and strive for those "wow" moments. Just don't be too quick to highlight those delightful moments, especially if it originated from an experience that was caused by friction. These high friction moments should have been prevented in the first place. Try not to highlight the step forward if you had to take two steps back to be able to take one step forward.

Most customers want you to help them fix their issues, they don't necessarily want to be delighted. They just want to get their issue resolved and go back to what they were previously doing or go to the next task they have on their list. Often times, even the simplest customer service interaction, is perceived as a chore to the customer. This is why you will see a spike in volume at lunch time, right after work, or on Sunday when they are running errands. If you dig into those interactions, you might find that the customer expectation is different than the rest of your callers. These customers might be quick to wanting a resolution and less appreciative of a surprise and delight experience. Depending on time of day or type of customer calling you might want to change up your support strategy. This is called customer segmentation.

What about FCR (First Call Resolution)? FCR seems like an important KPI to track the customer experience but can be extremely misleading. If you have a high FCR percentage in your contact center it might be really good or really bad. Of course, having a low FCR is not bad no matter what, but measuring FCR without measuring effort or friction can be misleading. If you have an environment where you force people to call in to do transactional calls, like reset a password or update profile information, of course your FCR will be high. Agents can handle these types of inquiries in their sleep. Doesn't this cause a high level of effort or friction? Shouldn't you try to deflect or self-serve these transactional interactions? If you removed all of these transactional interactions from your FCR percentage, what would your true FCR be? How much lower would your cost be due to lowering your required staff? How much staff occupancy would you free up in the day to day workload? These are all important factors to measure and change.

Another key friction point is the time it takes to resolve an issue. Some contact centers have problem solving or troubleshooting cases that take a long time to resolve. These contact centers have very few transactional inquiries and have to rely on tracking the progress of a case or ticket on behalf of the customer. A great example of this is the support provided by software providers. They aren't able to make a code change or fix a bug quickly, instead they have to generate tickets to track the bug or feature and wait till a development team releases code to resolve it. If you have one of these contact centers, I'm sure this is sounding very familiar by now. A huge friction point for contact centers like this, is the time to resolution. If you take a perceived longer than required amount of time resolving these issues it can start to deteriorate the customers view of your service and support. Service providers in this environment have SLAs (Service Level Agreements) to reassure the customer that they will be supported in a timely manner. Designing proactive communication for these environments can really help reduce friction. Dominos created a pizza tracker on their mobile apps and websites, so you know exactly where the pizza is. This reduced friction to their customers and prevented them from calling the location to check on the pizzas status.

On a much smaller scale, this same perception can be applied to wait times. If the customer has an easy issue, they might not be willing to wait a longer amount of time than if they had a harder issue. Take for example; the amount of time you are willing to wait to buy something at a retail store vs. the amount of time you are willing to wait to return or exchange a product at a retail store. Of course, in both scenarios you want it to be as fast as possible but purchasing something has a much lower perceived level of difficulty than doing an exchange. Generally, a checkout line of 5 people will move faster than a return/exchange line with the same amount of people. When you are in a checkout line you start to get impatient faster than when in a return/exchange line. When customers finally get to the front of the line, they could expect a higher level of service since they already invested so much time into waiting to be serviced. If you can do skills-based routing to separate these 2 (or more) types of customer intents, it can really reduce the friction and reset the customers perception.

Much like the time to resolution, the number of required times the customer has to contact you can cause friction. An example of this is having a specific time of the month where a customer has to call in. This is usually related to companies that have monthly or annual memberships. When they require customers to call in to resolve something regarding their renewal. The more you force your customers to contact you the higher the amount of friction. If you have the ability to enable them to only call or contact once instead of regularly, the better your customers will feel. This is the same for having cases or tickets (like I mentioned before) that require them to contact multiple times to get an update on their case/ticket status. If you can give them a portal to view this data on their own or email them regularly with status updates, this can reduce the amount of times they have to call in asking for an update. This creates less friction and an overall better experience.

Tier or level 2 support can be a very valuable tool for your contact center. What you want to be careful of is creating rules and policies that force customers to have to speak to a higher tier to resolve their issues. Empowering your front-line team members to resolve issues by themselves can drive down the friction that your customers experience. Imagine calling in to an insurance agency and having to be transferred to a manager (or tier 2) to resolve a simple insurance issue. It's that additional effort that makes that experience unpleasant.

How can you change your customer experience to reduce possible friction? What are the things you are doing today that can be defined as customer obsessed? If you had a magic wand, what *frictionless experience* would you create? Are there ways to slowly get to that goal by taking a phased approach? Who owns the customer experience at your company? Is it a group/committee of people or an individual? Do they meet regularly to make changes? What would they write on their post-it note, a customer facing capital E? These are all questions you should contemplate and answer to drive towards a more *frictionless experience* for your customers.

10

WFM and Staffing Practices Gone Wild – The Power of One

When I decided to go to college, like any junior in high school, I had no idea what I wanted to my major to be. I enjoyed math and ironically hated English. I was highly interested in technology as the internet was just starting to form its own identity. Simple computer programs fascinated me, and I was intrigued by the blank canvases that were created by websites like MySpace or Facebook. This was a time in my life where I had no idea what my career would be and everything new was an interesting discovery. This was a time before you could Google an answer for something or simply look at a Wikipedia page for reference.

The one thing that really caught my attention was *efficiency*. How to take a complex problem and make it simpler or faster. Things like, organizing my closet so I had types of shirts categorized and color coded. I knew exactly where my green long sleeve was in case I was in a rush to get to school. Turning the hangers, the other way on the closet bar if I wore that shirt in the last month so I knew not to be an "outfit repeater" by wearing the same outfit multiple times. All of these little efficiency tricks fascinated me while I was growing up, and little did I know that it would help develop me into the person I am today.

For college, I decided to major in Industrial Engineering, not the most commonly known major, and often confused with Mechanical Engineering (designing of mechanisms and parts). Even today when I describe my major to people who ask, I have to follow up with an example to clarify. In my opinion, Industrial Engineers are individuals who analyze and understand a workflow or process and make it more efficient - less costly, take less time, and hopefully increase productivity. This can be done with physical assembly lines, computer programs, contact center call flows, batching products together for order fulfillment... the possibilities are endless. What I learned in college is that Industrial Engineering isn't necessarily something physical, often times it is a mindset to solving business problems.

This experience, and my strange obsession with efficiency in workflows, is what fascinated me with contact centers. Starting out as a front-line technical support team member taking calls, I found obvious patterns emerging and commonalities that weren't very efficient. I noticed times where I was extremely occupied with calls while other times I was sitting idle. I enjoyed my 9 to 5 schedule but knew that on certain days of the month/week my coworkers would benefit if I came in a little early or stayed a little later. It wasn't until the contact center grew to about 25 agents that I learned about Workforce Management (WFM). It was the first problem I tried to solve, for my quickly growing customer service team, that elevated me into my first Team Leadership role. Without the opportunity to solve for scheduling and staffing needs, I don't think I would have had the career path that lead me to where I am today.

All of this new technology and process came with a steep learning curve. The first couple of months schedules were unstable and we were learning from some common mistakes and assumptions we had made. Things like allowing staff members to have rigid schedule preferences and forcing customers to contact us during open ours instead of 24/7. We did things like, only have two 1-hour lunch times (starting at 12 and 1) instead of having dynamic lunch times that could be 30 minutes or an hour long and start at any time of day. All of these WFM practices we could have potentially avoided. Hopefully in this chapter I highlight some other poor WFM staffing practices that you can avoid so you don't stumble on the same hurdles we encountered in the early days. Disclaimer; every contact center is different, please make sure you customize your WFM practices to match your staff and business needs as there isn't a one size fits all solution.

A direct result of your specific WFM environment can be your agent morale/satisfaction. It can help drive it up or down depending on their preferences. This is why it is extremely important to make slow calculated changes and involve the team on the designing and brainstorming process. One of the top reasons why people quit or change their careers is due to work schedules that don't match their preference or needs. You never want to lose talented people due to unmatched schedule preference. At the same time, your business needs to be efficient and productive. The challenge is to find the perfect balance of both.

Workforce management (WFM) and optimization (WFO) are an essential part of every contact center. The three key foundational technology pillars for every contact center are; IVR/ACD, CRM, and WFM. From a partner and tooling standpoint it is always important to choose these first, as your foundation, to run a successful customer service team. It is important to make sure the WFM process is just as good as the tool used to support it. I have seen best in class WFM technology utilized with some very restricting policies and procedures on-top of it. This completely defeats the purpose of using a WFM tool. It is designed to be flexible and give you the best forecasted outcome to your staffing needs. In this chapter we will go over some best and worst practices that can help optimize or hinder your workforce.

The most important thing is to start with is forecasting. When trying to forecast your required staff you should follow some basic rules of thumb.

- Choose intervals that work for your business - 15, 30 or 60 minutes are standard.

- Choose a service level objective that fits your needs. Don't pick one that is too aggressive or passive.
- Keep your forecast accuracy within 5%. When forecasting, make sure you have a +/- 5% accuracy compared to your forecasted volume.
- Project potential growth with volume drivers to forecast the future volume appropriately. Keep in mind that business changes can sway your standard forecasting models up or down.

The key drivers behind determining headcount staffing needs are; contact volume, service level agreement objective (SLA) and Average Handle Time (AHT). It is important not to manually manipulate these metrics when creating your initial forecast. It is very tempting to modify these metrics to try to lower the potential headcount needs and save money. It is crucial to not modify these metrics just to change the potential output of headcount needs. Instead, try to create forecasted scenarios (based off of all 3 of these metrics) that fit your budgetary needs. Once you have the right scenario created, make changes to strive to lower contact volume, SLAs or AHT. I recommend starting with current state and set goals for a more efficient future state later. As opposed to creating a headcount plan off of an ideal dream scenario and never hitting goals or SLA as a result.

Dynamic scheduling is an amazing way to leverage your team to its fullest. If you have a slightly larger group of agents on one type of skill (above 50) you can create a schedule that is more dynamic than rigid. Instead of having teams (groups of 10) mirror their team leaders schedules, you can have some (or all) of those teams scheduled dynamically and independently from their direct team lead. This means that they can be supported by any team leader during their shift and have a couple of hours of overlap with their direct team lead for feedback and quality assurance meetings. This is most effective with multiple teams, as it enables more flexibility in leadership coverage and scheduling. In this environment you could even leverage split shifts (agents with a 4-hour block in the morning and one in the afternoon) or 4 by 10 shifts (4 days scheduled with 10 hours per day). You could gain some efficiency on physical workstation space too. If you have agents spread across more dynamic schedules, you could do workstation sharing and prevent the need for physical space and the cost associated with it sitting idle and wasted.

Another WFM option is **pooling vs. dedicated swim lanes**. This is the routing methodology that can help you with your scheduling. The most common methodology is **pooling** (or Universal Agent). This is the strategy, that everyone is in the same "pool" and can handle any contact that comes in. You can do skills-based routing with this to clarify what agents are proficient in specific skills within that "pool". This is more commonly described as a **dedicated swim lane** model. Think of this as a community pool with swim lane markers to help separate swimmers. They still can go outside their lane, but they are the most proficient when they stay within their roped off areas. Both methodologies work, but dedicated swim lanes (skills-based routing) can be leveraged to blend or un-blend teams based off of proficiency. If you have drastically different queue and caller intents, you might have a less blended model, while similar queue and call intents would have a more blended approach. Here is an example; you might want sales and support to be completely separate, while your implementation teams can answer either type of call. In this example you might even have a couple of sales, and a couple of support blended as well. See 10.1 below for an example of skills-based routing blend for this environment.

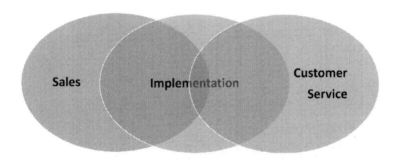

Figure 10.1 Skills-based Routing Blending Agents

When you have a WFM tool and process in place it can sometimes seem a little frustrating for agents.

They might dislike how rigid some of the rules are in dictating their schedule. It is important to remember that these policies and tools help make scheduling fair between all agents and remove scheduling bias or favoritism. You can program things like performance or tenure to gift your more experienced team members the ability to choose the schedule of their preference. Often times with a manual schedule you get preferential treatment and the business bends to the agent's schedule preferences vs scheduling based off what the business really needs. It can be difficult getting agents to work within these parameters, I would recommend putting the details of how scheduling works into the job description, so it is a condition of their employment.

If your WFM tool has the ability for agents to view and request schedule changes it might help with the adoption of WFM into the contact center. Enabling features like **schedule swaps** and **PTO requests** are great ways to enable self-service for your team. I recommend using this self-service portal to update them on any changes that might come up. Another great tool is overtime notifications. You can post upcoming overtime shifts or hours so that your team can log in and pick up those shifts/hours without having to talk to a WFM admin.

Giving agents a rolling published schedule ahead of time can also alleviate agent frustration and confusion. A rolling schedule is where you have the next

X weeks published for every agent. As the week comes to a close, the next x+1 weeks schedule gets published. I've seen companies publish 3 week rolling schedules as a more aggressive workforce optimization practice. If you publish a longer rolling week (like 8 weeks out) you have less flexibility, but higher agent satisfaction because they can plan vacations and time off farther out in advance. You can do this with monthly schedules too, but it creates another layer of complexity. Monthly publishing usually is done mid-month for the upcoming month. Publishing the next months (full schedule) on the 15th of the previous month.

WFM is a process first then product second, methodology. Remember that the WFM tool you use should not dictate your workforce optimization business needs. It should be the other way around. Business process and needs come first, and the tool should be dynamic enough to be customized to fit those needs.

Remember to factor in shrinkage, sick/PTO, and non-productive time into your forecasting models. These are humans you are scheduling, not robots. They will need bio breaks (bathroom, coffee, and water breaks), along with time for coaching and training. You should consider the team meetings and compliance training that is required to round out the rest of your agent's schedules. Another commonly forgotten metric is occupancy. This is the amount of time you could be occupied with work tasks during your shift. This metric should hover around the 70-80% range and never exceed 90%. If it gets too high than your agents don't get those natural "breather" moments throughout the day. If it is too low than your agents are most likely sitting idle between calls/chats and you are potential wasting money. If done properly you will find that less than 50% of your workforce's time is actually used to do productive work. At my previous company I have seen the total productive time to non-productive time forecasted to be in the 45-50% range. This seems inefficient, but if you are too aggressive with your staffing forecasts you will start to see agent moral drop and even see agent turnover.

It is important to constantly monitor and QA your IVR data as it is the backbone of your forecasting models within your WFM tool. Monthly audits are important to ensure data integrity for key metrics like Average Handle Time (AHT) and contact volume. A separate monitoring should be done at the interval level (more real-time) to assess whether or not you have the required staff for that interval. If you are getting less volume than expected in the beginning of the day you might see an unforeseen spike in volume later in the day to round out your daily average contact volume. You might see queues backing up due to AHT being higher than expected. This could cause a backlog or domino effect to your contact center that will change the rest of your days outcome. These can occur because of customer preference. Maybe there is a worldwide event earlier in the day that pushes them to contact you at a later time. If you can automatically push or pull data from your IVR/ACD tool it helps remove manual work and human error. This is one of the more foundational integrations that will support your entire contact center.

Having a fine balance between automated and manual WFM tool-sets is important. Some WFM products have features that automate the majority of the forecasting and scheduling. Even tools to automate the real-time dashboards and adherence. These are valuable tools and should be used. It is equally important to do manual checks (either within the product or external) to cross check the tools accuracy. This manual auditing process can help you validate that the data is correct and prevents errors that can cost your company large amounts of money or over/under staffed time periods.

Long term forecasting is just as important as short or mid-term forecasting. It is a fluid process that needs to have checks and balances. It is easy to be only focused on real-time or short-term staffing needs and to completely neglect long term forecasting. If you have a contact volume that is hard to forecast daily or weekly, it is valuable to validate against your long-term forecast. A smooth running WFM team updates and modifies long and short-term forecasts regularly. It's a living process that often gets updated weekly.

Schedule adherence is extremely important to monitor and coach against. A productive contact center may also have WFM team members who monitor and manage this in real-time. There is a fine line between having to police agents and educating them on the importance of schedule adherence. A good strategy for this is to provide agents with "The Power of One" training. This is a training that highlights how impactful a single agent off task can make the rest of the team strained with work as a result. You can do some fun exercises with your team to help illustrate this and foster better teamwork. The best team building I have done in the past is by setting up two equal lines of agents. Give all of the agents on one side a tennis ball. Let them throw the ball back and forth to the other side to represent a call. Each time it goes back and forth is like a conversation between the agent and customer. Now start removing people from one of the lines and tell them that it is because they are on break or not adhering to their schedule. They still should be throwing balls back and forth (but will feel short staffed). They will have to balance multiple balls and conversations at once, to cover for their out of adherence coworkers. You should start to see some dropped balls and agents frantically trying to keep up. After the exercise, it is good to pull the group together and allow them to share their experiences. This is a great and fun way to build buy-in into **schedule adherence** without making them feel policed in real-time.

To illustrate the potential impact of **schedule adherence** into staffing you should use the Erlang C staffing calculator (there are free ones online) to help visually calculate your ASA (Average Speed of Answer) values if you had less staff adhering to their schedule. See 10.2 below for an example of this.

Number of Staff	ASA (sec)	ASA (min)
54	6	0.1
53	8	0.1
52	12	0.2
51	19	0.3
50	30	0.5
49	50	0.8
48	91	1.5
47	236	3.9

Figure 10.2 Erlang C Staffing Calculator Example

As you may notice going from 54 to 53 agents only increases your ASA by 2 seconds. Going from 48 to 47 increases by 145 seconds (2 minutes and 25 seconds) and raised the total ASA to almost 4 minutes. This is a huge potential impact on the level of service you are delivering to your customers. This is a concept that is hard for agents to realize, especially as the team gets bigger. It is very common for an agent in this environment to say something like; "there are 50 other people working today. I will just go grab some coffee really quick, no one will even notice I am gone." Imagine if half of your staff did that at the exact same time. Your ASA and queue times would drastically increase as a result. This is why it is important to educate your team on the impact they all make.

WFM isn't just for inbound support contact centers. It can be applied to other business units (like sales) and outbound teams. I've seen it used for back office workers, who manage escalation queues and manager approvals. It can be used for live customer interactions (phone and chat) along with time-based responses (cases, tickets and email). As the support channel landscape grows, it is valuable to try to apply these best practices and methodologies to these emerging channels (social and voice assistants like Alexa). You can even utilize tools like call back and click to call to help push volume during busy to less busy times.

Not all of us are WFM gurus or have experience with Industrial Engineering best practices. I personally have only scratched the surface of WFM and WFO in my professional career. It is important to hire the right types of people to oversee this area of business. If done correctly it can save you a lot of money and headaches over time. Not to mention help display the value you offer to the greater company. An efficient team is a key to any company's success. That is why I value WFM as one of the most valuable parts of the contact center. If you need to hire a WFM manager/director or select a vendor partner, make sure to take your time and choose the right person. You don't want to suffer in this area. If you are an Industrial Engineer like me, you will find that any math heavy process is actually a work of art and needs a human component to be successful.

11

Know your Customers Multiple Personality Profiles – Persona Based Routing

Persona Based Routing is something that has been around for a while. NASA first designed it for the Apollo missions as a way to identify if certain personality types would communicate well in high stress situations. Like life or death situations while confined to a small space in a rocket ship reentering orbit. Imagine if 2 of the 4 people in that capsule had unhealthy communication or too lengthy of a conversation in that moment. Those conversations need to be efficient and without conflict.

To solve this issue, psychologists were hired by NASA to create groups of personas for every person. The goal was to match their compatibility and incompatibility traits. Some of these desired outcomes were; time to resolution of conflict, sentiment of participants after a conversation and overall trust with the other individual. These are all similar to the same contact center metrics and outcomes we try to produce; AHT, CSAT, and LTV.

What they found is that everybody fits into 6 different personality types. Some of these personality types work better with others towards these 3 different KPI goals. They found that some personality types can work better with multiple other types while some only work better with their own personality type. For example; a **creative** personality (Artist, Designer, Small Business Owner) might not have quick conversations with an **advisor** personality (Accountant, Lawyer, Architect). While that same **creative** type might be better matched with a **connector** personality (Counselor, Consultant, Therapist) type.

Online dating algorithms are designed off of these similar models. They take specific data points and categorize you based off of personality traits to match you the highest potential match. Personality matching has a higher success rate than any other data set for these types of companies. As odd as it seems, matching customers to agents is no different. Calls in a contact center can often feel like speed dating. Individual quick experiences with a different person each time that hopefully turn into positive results. Although setting your agents and customers up on dates isn't the goal, matching them so that they both have delightful experiences may be the desired outcome.

One of the most valuable exercises a contact center can do is separate their customers in to segments. Grouping or binning your customers by unique profiles can help you understand why some customers are outliers with specific KPIs. You might find that some of your customers are heavy spenders while others are onetime spenders. Some might cause longer talk time while others have short talk time on average. Most of these attributes are not random, they are trait specific to the customer based off of their unique habits.

Ideally using a Machine Learning tool is the best way to help identify your different customer personality profiles. These can be bought from a vendor or be developed internally for better customization. If you don't have the ability to implement a Machine Learning tool, you can always start simple by taking some key KPI data on your customers and separating them into groups. The simplest way to do this is by LTV (Lifetime Value). If you know the customers potential value, you can do things like route to agents faster (so they don't have to wait) or route to a more skilled agent. Another fun exercise is to find types of customers that have high AHT (Average Handle Time) and group them together. You can route these customers to agents who are better at handling longer conversations or agents that have more time left in their shift. It's not ideal to route a potential 1-hour call to someone who has 5 minutes left in their shift.

One of the more interesting methods is to separate based off of customer personality. This can be by segmenting them into non-business related segments and then correlating business KPIs after. Separate customers based off of; age, geography, sex, race, language, tenure as a customer, mobile or computer, family status, etc. then once you have a couple of personality types separated (between 4 and 8 types of customers) you can correlate those personality types to KPIs and predict outcomes. For example: a young female with no children who lives in a metropolitan city might spend more money on yoga classes than an older female with children who lives in the countryside. Another example is; a young male who lives in metropolitan city will want to talk faster (because he is on the go) than an older female who has 4 children (because she isn't as fast paced). See 11.1 below for an example of separating customers by personality profiles.

Connector	Organizer	Advisor	Original
Mid-size City	Major City	Small Town	Countryside
Compassionate	Logical	Observant	Creative
Wants to Relate	Wants Structure	Wants to be Right	Unstructured
Long Talker	Quick Talker	Medium Talker	Long Talker
$$$	$$$$	$$	$

Figure 11.1 Personality Profile Example

There is no perfect way to do this, it usually is a blend of subjective and quantitative data points. Even at the simplest level you will start to see trends between profile groups. Once you refine these group and identify the key drivers, leverage this information for routing, support and sales initiatives. You might find that a specific segment of your customers has the potential to spend more, or purchase if the product was a lower price point. Airline websites do this all of the time. If you look at airline prices from a specific location, they might be lower based off your location. Prices might be higher if you are searching while in a city vs if you are in the country. They sometimes change prices by weekday as they know customers don't purchase tickets for travel on certain days. Tuesday's are the days when Airline tickets are the lowest for consumers to buy. This is because consumers often don't plan leisure trips until the weekend. Monday's and Tuesday's (for Americans) are the days where you are returning back to work and usually occupied with errands and setting up the rest of your work week. This doesn't mean that people don't plan vacations on Tuesday's, just that the majority of us plan these trips on Thursday's - Sunday's. It is beneficial for the airline companies to increase pricing for those cohorts/segments of customers to increase their incoming revenue.

Here are some categories to consider when creating a persona profile for your customers;

>**Personal Demographics** - age, family (single, married, children), education, city, state, sex, ethnicity.

>**Monetary Values** - average income, spending habits, income to debt ratio, liquid cash to investment portfolio.

Physical Demographics - height, weight, clothing sizes, shoe size, hat size.

Personal Shopping Preferences - product likes and dislikes, types of past purchases, food/flavor palate, shopping location (online, in store).

Support Preferences - channel preferred, support time of day, length of call/chat or email response time, language, type of agent (male or female).

Customer Value - membership level, lifetime value, total spend, customer tier, rewards or loyalty level, customer referral/reach.

Communication Type - communication style (passive, aggressive, manipulative, passive-aggressive and assertive), PCM personality type.

PCM (Process Communication Model) personality types as designed by NASA;

Harmonizer - Compassionate, sensitive and warm. Joy from the movie "Inside Out."

Thinker - Organized, responsible and logical. Spock from "Star Trek" and Adrian Monk of the TV show "Monk."

Persister - Dedicated, observant, conscientious. Sherlock Holmes and Superman, as well as civil rights activist Martin Luther King, Jr.

Imaginer - Calm, imaginative and reflective. Superman's alter ego, Clark Kent, and genius Albert Einstein.

Promoter - Adaptable, persuasive and charming. James Bond and Ethan Hunt from "Mission Impossible."

Rebel - Spontaneous, creative and playful. Merida from the movie "Brave" and Robin Williams.

Traditionally IVR/ACD tools route based off of; the oldest caller to the agent who has been available the longest. This is commonly known as FIFO (First In First Out). Some more advanced contact centers do skills-based routing (like I mentioned in previous chapters). Skills-based routing takes the traditional routing, oldest caller to longest available agent, and combines it with skill proficient agents, allowing you to route based off of customer call intent or type. Most skills-based tools allow you to accelerate or decelerate certain skills over one another. While skills-based routing is a better routing strategy than having nothing at all, it still isn't the "best in class" solution. With medium to large sized contact centers, there are too many large skills that can be optimized and leveraged to create the best possible customer to agent match. With Persona Based routing you can match the best customer to agent regardless of their position in queue. It can calculate their potential business value and route them as a VIP to the best agent, who is available. Think of it as a personal car service, like an Uber, where skills-based routing is like public transit, a bus or train. It cares about the individual as opposed to just treating you like everyone else.

The next step is to design a routing strategy catered to these customer segments. This is the idea of matching a customer calling (or chatting/emailing in) to the agent that will produce the most desired outcome. This can be off of; lowest handle time, best customer experience (CSAT), highest sales potential, best save potential, etc. To do this successfully you will need to match a member profile information with agent profile information. The member segmentation data should be a little easier to define and track as most contact centers have a CRM with all of the customer data. The difficult part is correlating and weighing this robust data together to come up with some sort of **customer segment score**. The agent data is harder to create as in most contact centers, there usually isn't a CRM that houses all agent performance data. This is data like; agent tenure, proficiency, skill level, average handle time (AHT), etc. The end goal is to create a **customer segment score** (in your CRM) and match it to an **agent segment score**. When combined, these two scores should output a confidence rate on how likely the matched people will succeed towards the goal. See 11.2 below for a Routing Strategy based off of Confidence Rate and Customer Value Score.

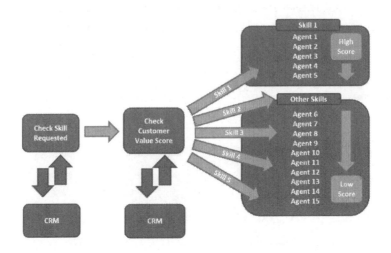

Figure 11.2 Routing Strategy based off of Confidence Rate and Customer Value Score.

When coming up with a Routing Strategy, really focus on what your specific business goals are. You can usually deduce this from your teams Mission or Vision statements, if they already exist. Does your contact center want to drive better experiences or quality? Lower costs or increase efficiency? Or produce more sales and lower attrition? The answer might be yes to all of the above. The goal is to find which one of those areas is the highest priority. If you need a blended model that supports multiple goals, try to design a routing strategy that allows you to dial (like knobs on a control board) these **customer segment scores** up or down. For example: create 3 different Customer Segment Scores (Quality, Efficiency, LTV) and have them weighted 1 to 10 based off of aggressiveness (confidence rate returned).

Then adjust these dials up or down until you have the ideal outcome. Example: Quality - 8, Efficiency - 10, LTV - 5. This is where A/B testing comes in extremely handy. In my experience, this is something you should lean on internal or external Data Scientists or Analysts to create and maintain. If this seems too complex or hard, there are companies out there that specialize in this and have created products for contact centers. I would recommend engaging with one of those providers if this is beyond your team's capabilities.

You may be saying, "Wait a minute, if I have lower AHT won't my agents have to take more calls?" Or "What if this routes all angry customers to one agent?" These are all legitimate concerns, but you have to remember that you are trying to categorize, and route customers based off what is most optimal for the business. This may not be a negative outcome, for both the agent and customer. The best analogy here is to think of a bag Skittles. You have two agents who will be eating these skittles. Let's say one of them absolutely hates the taste of the purple Skittle (bad match - long Handle Time). With random call routing, it's like this agent is just picking a random Skittle out of the bag without looking. The agent will occasionally get a purple skittle. Now take that same bag of skittles and separate all of the Skittles by color and putting them into bowls. Now give that agent who hates purple Skittles the other bowls first and the other agent the purple skittles first. This would reduce the randomization of sending an agent the least productive match. In this scenario, there are still the same amount of Skittles being consumed, it's just matching, and un-matching based off of your criteria. The answer is yes to both questions above. Some agents will take more calls than before, but this is because the conversations aren't wasteful or full of unnecessary conflict. One agent might get all of the angry customers, but they might enjoy the challenge of dealing with a harder customer and are the best at deescalating or defusing situations in a quicker manner (consuming the purple Skittles first).

One of the major benefits to routing efficiently is improving your agents focus. When agents start getting routed specific types of customers and intents they become more focused and there is less swivel chair (changing from one task to another). This leads to happier and more productive agents. Maximizing productivity means better First Call Resolution (FCR) and decreased Average Handle Time (AHT). Customers benefit because they get answers from an agent that is more confident and an expert in that call type. Agents are happy because they naturally become masters of specific topic and their agent metrics start to improve.

With tools like this, your service dynamically changes to the demand. With all Machine Learning tool-sets, they have a tendency to report and write back to the original algorithm. This is how the algorithm learns over time. This means that you will be able to adapt to the changes of your customers or agents as they happen. If you have a spike in specific types of calls that causes one of these KPIs to change, then the algorithm will adapt and accommodate to that change. This means that there is little to no maintenance on the Machine Learning technology beyond the first implementation. With the exception of minor adjustments and adding/removing KPI data points if the business needs to add/remove any.

From a workforce workload standpoint, personal based routing doesn't require manually changing agents from one queue to another. This is done in real-time every time someone calls in. This can eliminate new hire licensing setup and any admin work around assigning them to a queue. What normally makes this so difficult, is that some contact centers have to rely on internal IT teams to make simple changes to the queue skilling for an agent. A Machine Learning tools can eliminate this and remove the back and forth to get you the most optimal results without manual work.

Last agent routing is now possible. This is the routing strategy that allows you to route to the last agent the customer spoke too (if it was a good experience). It is especially valuable if you have a support team that has cases or tickets that stay open for a duration of time. This allows the customer to not have to reexplain the situation again, because the agent can recall the last conversation without having to read through case notes. Or at least start to remember the caller while looking through the case again. This can lower AHT for the agent and potentially prevent them from trying to read case notes and talk to the customer at the same time (which can create bad customer experiences).

All businesses thrive off the strength of customer relationships. For most businesses, the contact center is the only human interaction your customers will ever have with your company. This makes these conversations extremely valuable and meaningful. The customers viewpoint on your service, both quality and efficiency, could dictate if they continue to give their business to you or go to one of your competitors. It can also affect your brand through word of mouth, positively or negatively. This is why persona-based routing is so valuable.

Real-time customer-centric routing based off of individual and persona data is the way of the future. As we progress into the roaring 20s (2020s that is) we will be in an age of smart routing, virtual assistants, and personalized service. This will become the norm and customers will measure companies against it. Who will do the harshest measuring and judging? You guessed it, your high value customers. You're either going to be playing in the game or sitting on the bench. This is your opportunity to really start innovating in this area. The longer the wait, the longer you will be sitting on that bench.

Even though we might not be in the business of

sending someone to the moon, or helping a two people match so that they can love each other to the moon and back, it can be just as valuable to match the right customer to the right agent. Interactions and service shouldn't be frustrating and full of friction. They don't have to be unpleasant and lengthy. They can be engineered for the most optimal result. Allowing us all to spend all of this new free time to sit back and enjoy our favorite Skittle flavor... as long as it isn't purple.

12

The Subjective vs. Objective Spectrum

Ever babysit or take care of a kid and catch them in a lie? Or see them use an excuse for something they obviously did? We all did it when we were kids too. It's all about learning the boundaries of what you can get away with and what isn't acceptable. This is routed in our social and psychological growth as children, that helps us learn the difference between right and wrong. It also helps us understand how we (as humans) track and observe the world around us. Some of these we track numerically and some we don't. Like how teachers count how many times you show up late to school. Or slightly harder to track things like; how much ice cream is too much for a kid to eat right before dinner. Too much ice cream may be different based off who you ask, the kid might think the whole gallon is alright to eat. More measurable items like attendance can be much clearer. Being late to school 2 times a week may not be acceptable. How the kid reacts in these scenarios dictates how you might want to react and coach moving forward. You could find that the kid is blaming others for giving them the ice cream. Or complaining about how school is too early, when they obviously stayed up too late every night. How would you coach them to improve? Would we accept those excuses? What is the best way to approach these situations?

The funny thing is that sometimes as adults we act the same way. Maybe not with ice cream and attendance at school, but with work related tasks and other adult responsibilities. Some of us still use the same tactics we learned as children to push the blame to someone or something else. As a leader, how do you measure and track these? How do you coach them and drive improvement? Do you identify when your team is using excuses? In this chapter I will arm you will the tools you need to identify where you and your team are on the **Subjective and Objective Spectrum**. What you can measure, define, and document for improvement. Who on your team is stuck in the vicious **Drama Triangle** and how to get them out.

Subjectivity and **Objectivity** are both important ways of thinking when it comes to the contact center. **Subjective** information is usually information that is based off of judgement, personal point of view, emotional opinion and interpretation. It can sometimes come with personal bias. **Objective** information is closely linked to analysis, fact based measurable and observable KPIs. Based off of those definitions, you would think **Objective** thinking is the best way to operate. The majority of the time it is, but it's also very valuable to use the **Subjective** data as well. It's that "gut" feeling that often is correct and doesn't need much data validation. Often times when you hear, "We operate a data driven business", this is in reference to making decisions based off of **Objective** data. What does that mean for your business? Do you need to be more **Objective** and less **Subjective**? How can you change the way your team thinks and operates?

While the combination of both is the most ideal, it is important to identify when you are using one more than another to make business decisions. For the contact center, it is more common to lean more towards the **Objective** side for business decisions. Not everything has to be carefully calculated and measured to be successful, especially if you have to make a quick decision. If you know (in your gut) that a specific decision is the right move, then don't waste the time to measure and calculate the potential successful outcome.

To better understand this spectrum, it is good to use visual charts to describe where your decisions are happening today. The **Subjective vs. Objective Spectrum** as I describe it below highlights different tools you can use to try to define some of the undefinable. It can be used for business decisions as a whole but is best used for specific areas like; agent coaching and agent performance management. See 12.1 below for an overview of the Subjective vs. Objective Spectrum.

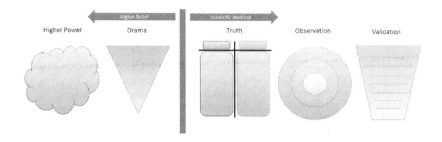

Figure 12.1 Subjective vs. Objective Spectrum

If you look at this chart, there are 5 key parts; 2 **Subjective** (to the left of the middle bar) and 3 **Objective** (to the right). I will describe these in detail starting on the left and moving to the right. The farther left the more **Subjective** and the farther right the more **Objective**. You can use these tools in conjunction with each other or use them independently. There isn't really a best practice, just a general awareness of where your team falls and how to potentially use these methodologies to create a more productive team.

Higher Power

- Karma
- Fate
- Luck
- Just Because
- Megan's Law

Figure 12.2 Higher Power

On the far left there is the **Higher Power** belief, which is the most subjective. Although similarly named, this isn't directly related to the belief of religion. It is loosely related, as it is the thought that things happen for a reason beyond your own control. Most agents will claim that things are happening because of things like; karma, fate, luck, just because, and Megan's Law. This is usually used by agents as an excuse when they perform poorly. It can be used by your leadership team when they don't have a reason for a positive or negative trend occurring. Some more creative departments or roles live and thrive in this area but contact centers (especially support) rely on **Objective** based decisions. Spikes in contact volume, increased average handle time, or strange contact arrival patterns might seem like they are unpredictable, but often times you will find some data driven reason that is causing these KPIs to change.

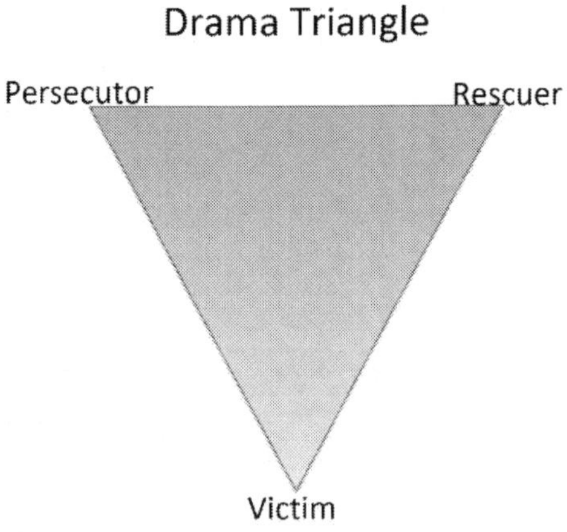

Drama Triangle

Figure 12.3 Drama Triangle

Next on the spectrum is the **Drama Triangle**, often described as Karpman's Drama Triangle. This is still on the subjective side of the spectrum as it is rooted in some subjectivity. This is where individuals explain (usually in a negative scenario) why something happened. A great example of this is when an agent is being coached on a specific topic (like schedule adherence).

This triangle has 3 points (personas); Prosecutor, Rescuer, and Victim. The Prosecutor is the person who is the root cause of the negative scenario. An example of this would be the Villain of the story. The Rescuer is the person who comes in to save the day, the Hero in most storybook tales. The Victim is the one who requires the saving. Usually the damsel in distress or main character in most Disney stories.

Like any good Disney movie some of your agents will play one of these roles. I've seen almost all of the three roles played out when attempting to coach a team member. Here are some common ones I've observed. Here are some examples of excuses used by Rescuers.

- Missed deadlines because they were helping other coworkers. Long handle time because they didn't want to hang up on customers.
- Not in the right phone status because they are doing wrap up work for a call that happened hours ago.

- Too much overtime last week because the phone queues were too large, and they wanted to help the team out.

All of these aren't desired agent behaviors and can seem acceptable because they are doing the "right thing". If you find the root reason (or why) that these agents are doing these behaviors, you will find that there is some personal gain out of it. Even though these seem like they are acceptable, they are really excuses of why they can't hit personal or team goals and should still be addressed/corrected.

When confronting and approaching an agent about performance you might get responses that place them into one of these 3 characteristics. For example; an agent might blame showing up late to work regularly on their carpool driver. This positions them as the Victim in this scenario. Or they might say they are late because they had to drive their kids to work. This positions them as the Hero. A less common reason is the Prosecutor role. An example of this would be the agent blaming the company for setting up such early schedules and how it is unfair for them to get to work with such a hard start time.

Each of these have personality traits that correlate to the roles. The Persecutor is similar to a bully; blames others, criticizes, dominating, puts others down for personal gain, angry and resentful, wants to lead or rule situations. The Rescuer is usually the martyr; strides to helping others for self-worth, selfless, feels the need to fix all problems, often few failures if others fail around them. The Victim is usually the person who feels helpless; hopeless, trapped, seeks out others to solve their problems, refuses to make decisions, dependent on others to succeed, will seek professional help (blame others when it isn't successful).

An agent who thinks and communicates with these traits often can't break out of the triangle. As the situation becomes more serious, they might move from one role to another in a toxic dance to remove themselves from responsibility or ownership in the problem. This is usually known as "excuses" or "gossip". This can be a vicious loop until they get their needs met. No actual concrete data is being discussed and this is why this falls to the left of the **Scientific Method** threshold.

The key goal when working with people who are stuck in this triangle is to get them out and help them get into the objective side of the spectrum. To do this you have to educate them on the triangle and use the phrases on the triangle to let them know what role they are playing in the moment. If you can get them to focus on the specifics details of why something is happening, then you might be able to break them from using excuses and owning the issue. The **TOV** model can help you break them out of this triangle and allow you to start having healthier conversations around opportunities. See 12.4 below for an example of the TOV model.

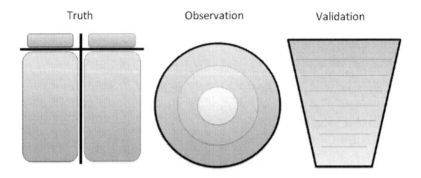

| Truth | Observation | Validation |

Figure 12.4 TOV - Scientific Method

The 3 tools for the **Scientific Method** are also known as the TOV model. This is due to the way you can visually write these charts and the initials to each section; **Truth, Observation**, and **Validation**. You can see the T, O, and V in black for each of these diagrams. If you use these (either in conjunction or individually) you will find specific details of why something is happening. When I have leaders wanting to put an agent on a PIP (Performance Improvement Plan) or formal coaching I require them to fill out a TOV spreadsheet. They need to define the **Truth**, prove they **Observed** the action, and **Validated** it with data. Without those 3, it is extremely hard to justify why a formal coaching is warranted.

Truth

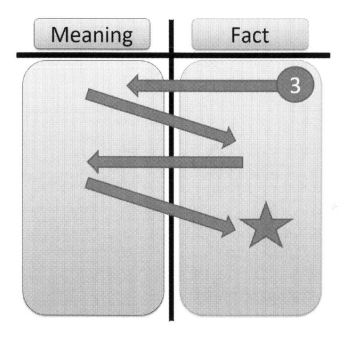

Figure 12.5 TOV - Truth

The **T** in this model is the **Truth** tool. It can be used to narrow down details until you find the actual fact behind a specific behavior or action. This is usually used as the 3rd and final tool in the **Scientific Method**. You start with a fact and move towards a meaning to describe why that fact happened. Often times this will give you another, newly discovered fact, which you then would derive the meaning behind. Repeat this until you find the underlining facts of why something happened.

An example of this would be the following;

1. **Fact** - an agent is late to work regularly.
2. **Meaning** - they can't adhere the schedule and could be put on coaching.
3. **Fact** - the agent carpools to work.
4. **Meaning** - they don't have control on their arrival time.
5. **Fact** - the carpool doesn't regularly leave on time.
6. **Meaning** - carpooling isn't a reliable form of transportation to work.
7. **Fact** - the agents carpool driver shift starts 1 hour later than the agents so there isn't a sense of urgency.
8. **Solution** - suggest the agent has to find a more reliable form of transportation to work.

Observation

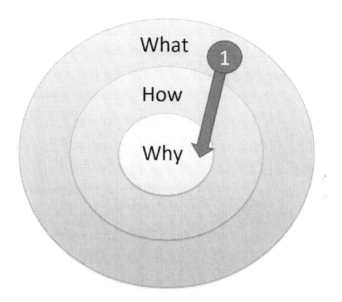

Figure 12.6 TOV - Observation

The **O** in the TOV model stands for **Observation**. This is usually the 1st tool you should use in this process. This is based off of Simon Sinek's Golden Circle (as I described this in a previous chapter). This is highlighted in his Ted talk "Start with Why" which is extremely informative, and I highly advise you watch. This is the methodology of observing your agent; starting with the **What**, then finding the **How** and eventually getting to the **Why** behind the behavior. Going off of the previous example, here is how to use this tool;

1. **What** - agent showing up late to work today.
2. **How** - measured them clocking in later than scheduled (in your WFM tool).
3. **Why** - agent's carpool driver dropped them off late to their shift.

Validation

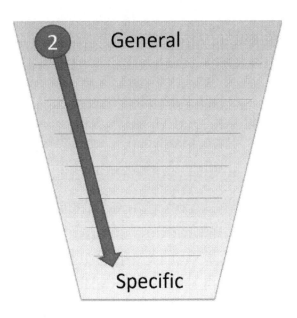

Figure 12.6 TOV - Validation

The final piece of the TOV model is the **V**, which stands for **Validation**. This is the process of taking some information or facts and making them more specific (instead of general). This is usually the 2nd action to take in the TOV model. In this step you can pull some relevant

KPIs to help highlight what behavior is happening. You take the **Why** from the **Observation** and determine if it is specific enough or too general. If it is too general, you have to ask questions to get more specific. Continuing with the example above, here is how you would apply this methodology;

General

1. Agent's carpool driver is dropping them off to work late.
2. The agent has no other form of transportation from home to work.
3. This is happening regularly.
4. This is every Monday and Friday.
5. The carpool driver works later on Monday and Friday.
6. Carpooling on Monday and Friday with this carpool will lead to the agent being late on those days regularly.

Specific

If you are using all 3 tools, try to start with the **Observation** then move to **Validation** and then **Truth**. If one of these areas is skipped or done out of order it can seem like a witch hunt. For example; if you try to **Validate** and then **Observe** it might seem like you are targeting a specific agent, just to get them in trouble. If you have already done the **Observation** and **Validation** in a previous coaching, then it might be alright for you to just jump to the **Truth**. This is a common practice for a second PIP (Performance Improvement Plan) or coaching check-in.

13

Scorecard Stretch Goals and Benchmarking Performance

One of the best things about sports is that there are plenty of KPIs and metrics that you can research on an individual or team. This is not only great information for spectators, but valuable for coaches, analysts and players. This information is the key factor that drives the player to become better at their sport. Baseball pitchers want to pitch a more perfect game. Soccer players want to score more goals. Football quarterbacks want to throw for more yards. Basketball players want to have a higher free throw percentage.

All of these KPIs help them measure their current metrics against benchmarks and set stretch goals for improvement. The same is true with your agents. They want to be the best, do better than the past, and improve over time. How can you create this environment without it being too competitive? What KPIs and metrics are within your agents control? When and how should you display this information to them? To have the best team out there, you have to embrace KPIs and provide visibility into these metrics to your team.

Through this process you might find out that not all of your agents are above the team's standards. This is where you have to decide to coach up or coach out. It is important to identify the team members who are efflcient and can also deliver a high level of quality. Some of your agents may fall below the average of the team regularly, it is important to try to coach or reposition them into other areas of the business. As John Maxwell said in his book *Developing the Leader Within*, "don't send your ducks to eagle school." This means a duck will always be a duck, it might not sore in the clouds with the other eagles. Remember that this might be ok. You might not need a team of eagles. You might only need a team of ducks. It is important to embrace the reality of situation and adapt if needed. This is why individual and team scorecards are so important.

Since the content of your scorecards are unique to each business, it is hard to advise on what to measure. Instead I will attempt to give you the framework of what is valuable (at a high level) for you to apply to your business. It's important to highlight who the audience is for each scorecard and make sure the goals/benchmarks are adjusted accordingly. I personally recommend having a dedicated customer service analyst (or team) to help support these scorecards, if you don't have them already.

Since scorecards have different audiences and purposes, I recommend putting together a master list and highlighting the different criteria for each. This matrix can help you stay organized with things like; data source, cadence, responsible analyst/owner, audience, purpose/goal, visualization method, and description. Once you have your plan, you can start designing each individual scorecard. See 13.1 below for an example of a Scorecard Planning Matrix.

Report Name	Goal	Report Owner	Requester	Recipients					Cadence	Priority	Data Source(s)	Visualization Method
				VPs	Directors	Managers	Agents	Workforce				
Executive Scoreboard	To inform the Executive team on overall performance of the contact center	Jane Smith	Jason Dec	x				x	Weekly	P1	ACD/IVR, WFM, CRM	Chart
Agent Performance Scorecard	To inform the site leadership team on agent and team performance	John Doe	Chin Jolen		x	x		x	Weekly	P1	ACD/IVR, WFM, CRM	Graphs and Charts
Site Comparison Scorecard	To inform the leadership team on which sites are performing compared to others	Jane Smith	Mike Jones	x	x	x		x	Monthly	P2	ACD/IVR, WFM, CRM	Graphs
Performance Based Pay	To inform the leadership team on performance pay recommendations for individual team members	John Doe	Alan Green		x	x		x	Quarterly	P1	ACD/IVR, WFM, CRM	Chart
Agent Performance (Individual)	To inform individual agents how they are doing in comparison to the rest of the team averages	Jane Smith	Mike Jones			x	x	x	Weekly	P1	ACD/IVR, WFM, CRM	Graphs and Charts

Figure 13.1 Scorecard Planning Matrix

One of the most valuable scorecards is the Agent Performance Scorecard. This can drive individual agent performance up and create some healthy natural competition. Much like a video game (or gamification) this can be leveraged to show where they are with regards to their peers and also allow them to see their individual improvement over time. You can use these metrics to provide bonuses, business perks, and even compensation. I get to that topic in the next chapter when I go over performance-based pay.

At everyone's core they want to inherently improve and do better. The question is, how will they know where they're currently performing and in what areas can they improve? Let's go back to the sports analogy. How does a baseball hitter know he is doing well? Is it the number of home runs, hits, walks? Is it a combination of all three? Maybe it is the number of pitches that the batter has seen (to wear-out the pitcher). How has the hitter performed in the past? Are they improving? Are others on the team doing better? The answers to all of these questions are best answered by their batting coach. But the conversation can't be productive without creating a clear understanding of all of these KPIs. The same is important for your agents. Visibility into these metrics and regular coaching sessions with their team leader can improve performance and the greater teams performance as a result.

I recommend starting with agent performance as a whole. Performance can best be measured between 2 buckets; Quality and Efficiency. If someone does something efficiently with a high level of quality, it usually means that they are a high performing agent. Quality can be a combination of multiple different metrics; CSAT (Customer Satisfaction), FCR (First Call Resolution), NPS (Net Promoter Score), CES (Customer Effort Score), CXS (Customer Experience Score), Escalations, QM (Quality Monitoring), etc. Efficiency can be measured with these metrics; AHT (Average Handle Time), Schedule Adherence, Occupancy, Show Rate, ASA (Average Speed of Answer), HT (Hold Time), etc.

Beyond including Quality and Efficiency into these agent scorecards is the other Performance category. This is unique to your business, but can be things like; Save Rate, Up-sell Percentage, Certification Level, etc. These are important to report and measure against to drive improvement over time.

Once these KPIs are grouped within buckets, it is important to weigh each section. Within each section weigh each KPI against each other. This will create an overall Quality, Efficiency, and Performance Score. These scores can be used to highlight areas of opportunity for improvement along with recognition for the best performers in each category. See 13.2 and 13.3 below for an example of a Performance Scoring and Ranking.

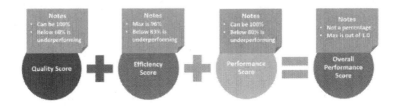

Figure 13.2 Performance Scoring

Name	Manager	Quality Score	Efficiency Score	Performance Score	Combined	Overall Performance
Gracia Muszynski	Nathan	80.00%	86.01%	91.06%	2.57	0.86
Waneta Timmerman	Jack	74.00%	92.37%	89.53%	2.56	0.85
Jamey Frantz	Jason	85.00%	86.90%	83.46%	2.55	0.85
Garnet Roby	Kate	72.00%	95.13%	87.96%	2.55	0.85
Camille Olenick	Nathan	90.00%	72.71%	81.16%	2.54	0.85
Kym Eckman	Jason	80.00%	89.18%	82.97%	2.52	0.84
Afton Lemasters	Nathan	80.00%	85.77%	85.64%	2.51	0.84
Gertha Coupe	Jack	80.00%	92.61%	78.69%	2.51	0.84
Clayton Spraggs	Nathan	80.00%	84.46%	86.12%	2.51	0.84
Yasuko Drummer	Jack	73.67%	88.29%	86.38%	2.48	0.83
Agustina Lichtenberger	Graham	80.00%	84.39%	82.93%	2.47	0.82
Barbie Bonier	Jason	80.00%	85.32%	80.33%	2.46	0.82
Shonta Spiva	Lisa	75.00%	82.87%	87.35%	2.45	0.82
Lincoln Dawdy	Jason	75.00%	84.39%	84.09%	2.43	0.81
Allison Neely	Graham	70.00%	89.11%	83.99%	2.43	0.81
Tosha Grau	Kate	67.00%	89.11%	85.87%	2.42	0.81
Eva Fredricks	Lisa	75.00%	80.84%	85.67%	2.42	0.81
Jaclyn Pentz	Lisa	70.00%	85.06%	85.94%	2.41	0.80
Chin Barnwell	Graham	60.00%	90.10%	89.89%	2.40	0.80
Oneida Wand	Jack	65.33%	88.15%	86.49%	2.40	0.80
Argelia Rowe	Graham	70.00%	85.09%	84.72%	2.40	0.80
Jonathon Gideon	Jennifer	72.00%	86.67%	81.11%	2.40	0.80
Obdulia Cartier	Tony	65.00%	81.31%	92.61%	2.39	0.80
Ezequiel Ziolkowski	Kate	68.67%	88.97%	80.05%	2.38	0.79
Blanche Wineinger	Lisa	70.00%	84.08%	82.75%	2.37	0.79
Marna Knaack	Jennifer	63.50%	88.08%	84.26%	2.36	0.79
Herschel Shortridge	Jason	65.00%	90.18%	80.63%	2.36	0.79
Fran Layman	Graham	65.00%	84.42%	84.64%	2.34	0.78
Justine Hayashi	Jennifer	68.50%	82.88%	81.42%	2.33	0.78
Kirby Gantz	Theron	65.00%	81.63%	82.72%	2.29	0.76
Stan Kyler	Graham	50.00%	90.07%	86.09%	2.26	0.75
Jenifer Oles	Theron	65.00%	77.74%	82.81%	2.26	0.75
Stewart Lahey	Nathan	60.00%	82.76%	81.90%	2.25	0.75
Suzanne Helmuth	Nathan	60.00%	85.33%	60.17%	2.06	0.69

Figure 13.3 Performance Score Ranking

Another vital scorecard is the weekly Executive Scorecard. This is a collection of the same KPIs listed above but filtered by the team as a whole. The audience for this report is your customer service senior executive and/or leadership team. This is the scorecard that lets you know the health of the businesses last week performance in comparison to previous weeks or similar calendar week to the years before. Other than Quality and Efficiency KPIs, it is important to measure contact volume and self-service containment. If you can break contact volume by channel that is also beneficial. See 13.4 below for an example of an Executive Scoreboard.

	CW 9	CW 8	CW 7	CW 6	Feb	Jan	Last 90 Days	YTD	Last Year
Virtual Agent (Voice) Total Calls	286,194	115,988	260,085	231,314	893,581	1,086,743	2,339,412	1,980,324	6,348,582
Virtual Agent (Voice) Containment Rate	14%	12%	11%	12%	10%	11%	14%	12%	11%
Total Calls	329,181	181,261	342,685	326,091	1,233,941	1,243,701	2,606,266	2,477,642	7,781,467
Calls Offered to Agents	275,307	158,377	308,176	271,439	1,090,213	1,009,206	3,249,441	2,038,587	6,541,783
Agent Handled	254,278	149,307	281,718	254,894	1,000,875	932,150	2,034,692	1,854,247	6,013,772
Answer %	92%	94%	91%	94%	92%	92%	90%	91%	92%
Average Speed of Answer (ASA)	0:27	0:33	0:45	0:38	0:35	0:28	0:35	0:31	0:23
Service Level (SLA)	70%	38%	25%	33%	36%	44%	36%	41%	49%
Average Handle Time (AHT)	5:46	5:29	5:27	5:41	5:19	6:00	5:42	5:59	5:13
Save Rate	28%	26%	21%	33%	27%	31%	34%	29%	36%
CSAT Rating	88%	90%	91%	90%	87%	90%	86%	94%	93%
CSAT First Call Resolution	93%	94%	89%	90%	92%	86%	91%	91%	86%

Figure 13.4 Executive Scoreboard Example

If you have different groups of agents, separated by site or leadership styles, you can create a comparison guide. These comparison scorecards can show you how one team or group is working in comparison to others. We use Site Comparison Scorecards to measure the effectiveness of our different BPO sites. This allows us to hold our different support vendors to benchmarked standards and enables us to negotiate costs if the site is performing poorly. Even if you don't have BPOs, you can use this same technique to create standardization across sites, teams and even departments. In the example below, each graph is separated by a specific site. You can clearly see the differences in different quality, efficiency, and business impact. This is very helpful when deciding what team or site to continue to do business with. See 13.5 below for an example of a Site Comparison Scoreboard.

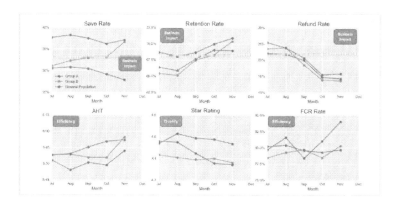

Figure 13.5 Site Comparison Scorecard Example

After implementing core scorecards like the examples above, it is important to use the correct methodology to create stretch goals and proper benchmarking. Only benchmark and create goals for metrics that are within the control of the contact center team members. Some KPIs are not good to set individual goals for. ASA (Average Speed of Answer), Contact Volume, and Occupancy are all KPIs outside of agents direct control. For KPIs that can be influenced by agent behavior I recommend starting with the average and taking standard deviations above and below the average. Some metrics should be lowered (lower control limit) while others should be increased (upper control limit). While some unique metrics should have both a lower and upper control limit and be measured against maintaining the average (or slightly above/below the average).

KPIs that can benefit by having a lower benchmark goal are usually associated to Efficiency and

Effort. The contact center can benefit by driving these KPIs down; AHT (Average Handle Time), HT (Hold Time), and CES (Customer Effort Score).

Most Quality and some Attendance KPIs should be driven by higher benchmark goals. Here are some KPIs that benefit from having a higher goal; CSAT (Customer Satisfaction), FCR (First Call Resolution), NPS (Net Promoter Score), CXS (Customer Experience Score), QM (Quality Monitoring), Show Rate, and Schedule Adherence.

14

Foster Employee Drive – Performance-Based Pay

It is human nature to want to do the best. Even when we can't achieve the best, we still have a natural drive to improve and do better. Especially in a contact center, where the majority of the team already has a high level of compassion and empathy towards customers. In the contact center our drive is to support whoever we are talking with, and continuously improve our unique ability to do so.

In the book *Drive* by Daniel H. Pink, he goes on to describe that what we traditionally know about motivation is actually incorrect. The carrot or the stick mentality, doesn't actually drive success. With the "carrot" approach; high bonuses or heavy commission on a job well done may slightly increase performance, but you might find employees trying to game the system to get higher pay with the same or similar work output and performance. Sales teams are known to sandbag sales forecasts, just so they can under promise and over deliver (for higher commissions in the end). The "stick" approach isn't much better. Punishing employees for not hitting metrics or goals with coaching or corrective meetings just demoralizes employees. These are short term solutions that don't actually increase the individual employees level of internal drive.

In his book, Pink highlights 3 different and unique reasons behind anyone's drive:

1. **Autonomy** - the desire to direct our own lives.
2. **Mastery** - the urge to get better and better at something that matters.
3. **Purpose** - the yearning to do what we do in the service of something larger than ourselves.

These are key to any employee's success. An employee needs to have the ability to not be micromanaged and allowed enough **Autonomy** to work on what they feel is important. This allows the employee to feel *bought in* to the vision or mission of the team or company. They need to be enabled to have **Mastery** in their roles. They need to become the best at what they do, so they can learn to grow beyond their current job and start down their long-term career path and goals. **Purpose** is one of the most important parts of this formula. This is the north star that points the employee in the right direction every day. Without this, you might see employees start to turnover or disengage in their work because they don't see (or align with) the team vision or mission. Think about major sports stars, artists, and even large technology CEOs; they all had/have these three key parts to **Drive** them to be the best at their unique area.

Performance Pay is a methodology that is rooted in this concept. It isn't just another way to compensate. It needs to have all of these elements to make it successful. Keep in mind that Performance is not only **Drive**, but also **Productivity** and **Quality**.

Think of an assembly line. You have a conveyor belt pushing a product from station to station to finally be completed. Let's take a shoe for example. The shoe starts off as multiple raw materials cut with machines. Then it is passed to an area where it gets assembled. Then to a station where it gets laces and details (like logos, colorful wrapping). Finally, it arrives in the packaging and boxing area where it is prepared for retail. For all of these to be successful they have to be done **Productively** (efficiently) or the line would back up and a pile of unfinished shoes would start to form at a specific station. They also have to be done with a high level of **Quality** otherwise the next phase of the assembly line can't do its task(s). Think about 2 left shoes reaching the end of the line for packaging. Sometimes you can sacrifice one of these traits to help the other. You can have a poor-quality product done quickly. Or inversely; a great quality product done slowly. This is where **Drive** comes in. The operator at the assembly line station (or contact center agent) needs to have the drive to make sure the product is produced with enough quality within the appropriate amount of time to align with the overall **Purpose**.

Applying this to the contact center team is rather easy. Focus on the KPIs and key metrics that can be measured on an agent level and compensate them for this. Ideally you should put these types of questions in your recruiting and training classes, so you get the right types of employees on your team to begin with. Everyone on your team should know these terms and should be talking about them when they meet with their leadership on a regular basis. I recommend putting these key areas in your yearly employee performance reviews.

When we rolled out Performance Pay in the support contact center floor we found that agents loved it. They no longer were being paid off of tenure and coached when they were slightly off on a KPI. Instead they noticed that their pay could be affected if their performance declined or improved in a specific area (like quality). This allowed agents to be more autonomous with regards to their pay and professional career growth. We found that some agents were content with doing just enough to get by, while others became naturally competitive to do better and be the best on the team. We embrace both types of employees on our team to keep the team happy and healthy. This is similar to the **Invisible Hand** theory that was invented by Adam Smith in his book, *The Wealth of Nations*. This states that there is an unobservable market force that helps demand and supply of goods in a free market to reach equilibrium. The same is true with **Drive** in your contact center; agents will naturally supply the higher performance if there is a demand for it in an open market.

Something interesting that we found was that tenure doesn't need to be factored into this pay model. Over time the agent would get naturally better at these areas and this got them higher compensation without having to add tenure to the equation. The agents, without a high level of performance and a long tenure, aren't compensated as highly as agents with high performance metrics (regardless of tenure). This does 2 key things; increases drive to improve quickly and prevents good agents from leaving because they felt like they aren't paid fairly based off of their smaller tenure. Ideally you want to pay your best performers the most, instead of just giving it to agents based off of warming the seat.

Whatever KPIs you pull into backing this Performance Pay formula; the key is to weigh certain areas to align with your business culture and mission. You might find that it doesn't need to be an even 1/3rd split between **Drive**, **Productivity** and **Quality**. See figure 14.1 for an example of a Weighted Performance Pay formula.

Figure 14.1 Weighted Performance Pay

Performance can be broken down with these objective measurements but remember that performance doesn't necessarily measure talent. Talent is something that can be natural or something that doesn't start to show until someone is in an environment where it allows it to thrive. Some customer service employees might not even know they are good at something like sales until you infuse that into their day to day. They might have the natural talent for selling. This is something that works in parallel with performance. Someone can be performing well due to the natural talent that they possess. Potential talent is a factor to keep in mind when thinking about your team and individual agents. If an agent isn't performing well I recommend looking into their potential talent. It might be valuable to keep them on the team and find the environment that leverages their natural talents. This can be an effective strategy if the goal is to reduce overall turnover for the company.

There are many different types of ways to pay employees. Ways like; commission, salary/hourly, and tenure (like how school teachers are paid in America). Performance-based pay is a hybrid of the traditional salary/hourly and commission-based pay. It takes the benefits from both systems. Salary/hourly employees get raises after their individual performance increases, usually on a yearly cycle. For each assessment (we did yearly) the agents performance pay would be calculated and changed to the new pay scale. This is unlike how a car salesman gets paid commission based off of each individual car sale. This promotes consistency performance improvement instead of single performance spikes or events. In football; the offense who can get 4 yards on average per play will always get a first down and eventually score. As opposed to trying for a hail mary (long pass) every play and hoping to catch it. Although it is entertaining to watch a hail mary, they aren't a productive way to regularly run an offensive football team. This is due to low likelihood of catching a hail mary. This is the same for call center agents. We want to drive them to have short calculated wins vs. incentivizing them to try to save customers every time. The small customer service experiences are the ones that will keep customers coming back.

Another positive byproduct of performance-based pay is that it removes the perception of favoritism. This helps make the employers expectations clear. Performance-based pay can allow good agents to stay in their roles and get paid as much as leadership. This removes the traditional thought of, "I have to become a team leader to get a raise." Paying agents their worth sooner may be costlier in the beginning, but it will retain them for longer which will benefit you, and the team, in the long term. The goal is to get high performing agents paid their worth sooner and preventing them from feeling underpaid. If the agent is continuing to perform at the high level, there is no need to continue to give a tenure-based raise. Notice that the performance-based pay agent gets paid more quickly and don't get raises once they become the best on the team. The tenure-based pay agent slowly gets increased based of off tenure, but never truly makes what they are worth (performance wise) until well beyond their 4th year. This will cause the tenure-based pay agent to either stop performing at a high level (because it has no value) or be frustrated at performing well but know that other more tenured underperforming agents are getting paid more. See figure 14.2 for an example of an agent being paid based off of Performance vs. Tenure.

Name	Pay Type	Starting Pay	6 Month Raise	6 Month Pay	1 Year Raise	1 Year Pay	2 Year Raise	2 Year Pay	3 Year Raise	3 Year Pay	4 Year Raise	4 Year Pay
Mark Johnson	Tenure	$10.00	3%	$10.30	5%	$10.82	5%	$11.36	5%	$11.92	5%	$12.52
Mark Johnson	Performance	$10.00	5%	$10.50	10%	$11.55	10%	$12.71	0%	$12.71	0%	$12.71

Figure 14.2 Performance Pay vs. Tenure

Drive is a huge motivating factor for agents. The biggest contributor for some agents is **Autonomy**. This is the ability to plan and dictate your own workload and schedule. People who are more of the creative type prefer more autonomy vs. more analytical types like structure and guidance. This of course is a generalization, but it often holds true when grouping your agents into personality types. With more autonomous agents, they need leaders that can adapt to their preferences.

In the 2010 movie comedy *Meet the Focker's* they talk about the Ferber Method vs. the Focker Method. "The Ferber method, or Ferberization, is a technique invented by Dr. Richard Ferber to solve infant sleep problems. It involves 'baby-training' children to self-soothe by allowing the child to cry for a predetermined amount of time before receiving external comfort." - Source Wikipedia. Whereas the Focker Method (as comically described in the movie) is the technique of over nurturing and coddling the baby/child to calm it down.

This can be a major factor into your agents experience as well. By no means are your agent's children, but how leaders treat them in the workplace can dictate their performance and drive. Too much coddling (also known as micromanaging) can lead to burn out or disinterest in their day to day job. Not enough support can feel like there isn't any guidance or leadership. A good understanding of your specific agents needs and balance between hand holding, guidance, and support is critical to the success of any team's drive. Don't create environments where **Autonomy** is stifled.

Another factor to **Drive** is the way your team is structured. It is important to allow your agents to be in a group/team/community where they feel like they can provide value. This is often lost when the team gets too big and voices or feedback fall on deaf ears. Size of the team can affect the internal drive an agent has into performing at a high level. Robin Dunbar, an anthropologist and evolutionary psychologist, came up with a science behind this phenomenon. Dunbar's Number dictates that individuals lose the personal connection (individual voice) when the greater group hits

150 people. As humans we have thresholds of how many people we connect with on these different levels. Outside of our personal core connects (immediate family and friends - usually about 5 core people) we have another circle of friends (around 15 people). Beyond that we associate with a group who we really trust (coworkers, loose friends, etc. - usually about 35 people). Beyond that we can only really keep and foster loose relationships with 150 people (the greater tribe). Anything beyond 150 people and it gets hard to maintain meaningful relationships. See figure 14.3 for an example of the Dunbar's Number Thresholds.

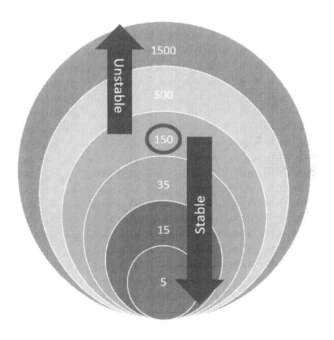

Figure 14.3 Dunbar's Number Thresholds

This holds true for contact center teams too. Think of an individual agent. They probably have 5 people they work with and completely trust (their inner circle and trusted coworkers). Sometimes their manager/leader is in this tight group of 5, but not always. Then they have a slightly greater group that they belong to. That is why teams of 15 (including their Team Leader) are the most effective. Beyond that, usually a couple of teams (2 teams of 15) grouped together can be effective at tackling almost any problem. We would often assign 2 teams of 15 agents to a topic that needed specific attention, instead of giving it to the whole team of 300. We called this method *swarming*. A stable contact center is a team of about 150 (including leaders and managers). This is about 11 to 13 teams of 11 to 12 agents with a leader per team and a manager of those 12ish team leaders. This is a highly functioning team that can operate individually from any other contact center team. You can have more in each contact center 'pod', but it starts to lose individual agent drive and motivation. If you have to have more than 150 per physical contact center, I would recommend trying to separate them into groups of 150. This allows them to relate to the stable group that they can belong to as opposed to it becoming unwieldy and unstable. Team names, physical separation on the contact center floor, and healthy competition are great ways to separate these groups without losing out on individual contribution and drive.

Team members in larger groups often feel like

they don't have a voice, and/or their task doesn't have high importance. This is a byproduct of the growing contact center environment. This is prevalent in assembly line type roles where there are long workflows. The team member may not be able to see beyond the 2 or 3 steps before and after them. We saw some frustration and disengagement for agents in these environments because they felt that they were just creating a ticket and then throwing it "over a fence" to the development team to solve. To empower agents in this environment you have to do a couple of things. It's important to educate them on the complete workflow and highlight the importance of their role in that workflow. Everyone in the workflow has value and understanding the big picture re-instills **Drive** into the individual employee.

Another method is to allow them to have an **Andon Cord**. An Andon Cord is a way for anyone in the workflow to be empowered to notify and escalate that there is a problem at their part of the workflow. For assembly lines this notification system can possibly stop the line because of some defect or quality deficiency up the assembly line. Without a notification system like this it can force poor quality product to move to the next station down the line and so on. These are also used in public busses, the yellow cords that run down the sides of the bus inside. If you pull these cords it lets the driver know to stop (supposed to only be used for emergencies). For contact centers it is important to empower your front-line agents with tools like these. It can be as simple as raising a hand or turning on a red light near their station to pull a leader over for support/validation. You can embed manager codes into your CRM and do this digitally instead of physically/manually. Another great use for this is in the retail product support space. If there is a problem or defect with a specific product the agent can take that product down from the website. Example: a popular shoe you sell has a defect in the stitching that wasn't caught before it was sold to customers. An agent might get multiple calls regarding this issue in a single day, identifying it as a defect that is affecting everyone who purchased this shoe. The agent should be able to immediately take that product down (and write a note why they took that action). By doing this you not only instill **Drive** and **Purpose**, but it can also positively affect the bottom line. It can reduce the cost of returning the products due to the defects and reduce future call volume (staffing costs).

It's human nature to want to do the best. We all have internal **Drive** to constantly improve. We all have the best intentions in mind when at work. We start to lose **Productivity** and **Drive** when we aren't aligned with the **Purpose**. Try to avoid hiring talented and putting them in an environment where they don't have purpose. This is a drive killer and will set them up for failure. Empowerment is crucial to the employee's success, without it they will feel their tasks are meaningless and mundane. Harness that internal drive within all of your employees and remove those rules/guardrails that prevent them from being engaged In their job. Most importantly; pay them for their performance, because they are worth it!

15

Customer Experience is based off of Employee Experience

I will always remember the worst customer experience I have ever had. It was when I had to return a cell phone at a store. I walked in and was greeted by someone who obviously didn't want to be there. They clearly hated their job and didn't care about anyone or anything. It was a painful 45 minutes where I had to lead the employee through what I needed while he expressed very little empathy or compassion. I left that store thinking; he must really hate his job and why would he continue working there? Even though I got my problem resolved, I thought less of that company's brand. I wondered what my money was going towards. I felt bad for the employee and wished I could help him.

Imagine you're working the phones in your contact center. You have taken your 25th call of the day. The last 10 have been so similar that you can't remember anything specific about them. It feels like the last 4 hours of your life was a pointless blur. You're hungry, sick of talking out loud, frustrated because you had to skip your morning 15-minute break. No one at work acknowledged you all morning except for the meaningless "good mornings" from your coworkers as you walked in. How are you supposed to be the face of your company to your customers in this type of environment? The quality of the work you do is directly correlated to how happy you are, especially in the contact center.

"You can hear a smile through the phone." How many times have we all heard this. If you run a contact center, this saying is as cliché as any other. I have even seen this on a QA scorecard where it was required for agents on every call. The question is, does this really work? Do you really get higher customer satisfaction from agents who are happy and smile through the phone? I'm a firm believer that; happy employees equal happy customers. I'm also of the belief that the opposite is true; unhappy employees equal unhappy customers. Negativity spreads like wildfire and is hard to turn that back into positivity.

Now that the customer has the ability to post their experiences on social media, it is even more important to always provide the best experience. These experiences can't be faked, customers will know when the agent they are talking to is faking it. Even if you have the best brand or product your customers can be unhappy with your customer support. They will mirror your employee's emotions and happiness. Below are studies that were done by Mobius, MetricNet, and Salesforce that explain this phenomenon. Each dot represents a different company. After surveying employee's satisfaction and customer's satisfaction, you can clearly see that happy employees produce happy customers. See figure 15.1 and 15.2 for charts on the correlation between Employee and Customer Satisfaction.

Figure 15.1 Employee and Customer Satisfaction - Mobius

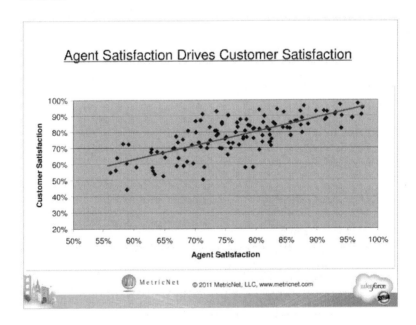

Figure 15.2 Employee and Customer Satisfaction –

MetricNet and Salesforce

This lead me to rethink how I want to lead my contact center and team. I wanted them to enjoy work, and truly enjoy helping others. I wanted them to wake up in the morning and want to come to work instead of dread it. I wanted them to feel safe, engaged, and comfortable at work without making it too stuffy or too relaxed. We now know that happy employees mean happy customers. If this is true, then what can you do to keep your employees happy? By focusing on my employees work experience and environment I found that the customer experiences improved.

Someone once said, "Love what you do, and you will never have to work a day in your life." The goal is to create an environment where employees don't feel like it is a chore. It should feel like an extension of home and coworkers should feel like friends. Since you spend the majority of your time awake at work, why do we make it so miserable. It might be a lofty goal to create an environment that all employees love, but it shouldn't be hard to at least make it a place they like to be.

"I believe in the power of recognition and empowerment leading to great employee engagement. And employee engagement is critical to guest engagement. Employee empowerment and recognition is the core of our culture and how we achieve outstanding customer service." Herve Humler, The Ritz-Carlton Hotel Company

Here are some of the ways you can improve the employee experience, so that they can come to work and truly, "love what they do."

Learning and training should be provided and encouraged:

Most employees want a company to help them learn new skills and improve the ones they currently have. If you encourage learning you will find that your employees will enjoy coming to work, because it feels like there is a direct investment into their future. This can be done ad-hoc with little organization or done with structure and/or gamification. I found that creating a school like curriculum (like majors and minors) creates the best employee engagement and feedback. Allowing them time to learn while they are at work is beneficial to both you and them. Initiatives like this can drastically increase the amount of time they stay with your company by reducing burnout. It can also teach them something relevant to their day to day work and result in a better customer experience.

Create engaging rewards and recognition programs:

Every employee wants to do well at work. They also want to be rewarded or recognized when they do a job well done. Not every employee wants public recognition. It is important to provide the recognition in the way that the individual want to receive it. Gamification and performance-based pay (or compensation) are great ways to reward employees. You can do it in simpler ways with badges, desk trinkets, stamp passports, etc. These programs don't have to cost large amounts of money or be too elaborate. We had weekly stand-up meetings (everyone stands at their desk) where we would start and end the meeting with recognizing a team member. When we did this recognition, we focused on a specific accomplishment they achieved in the last week. It had to be a genuine recognition, nothing that was generic or a stretch. Not only did this inspire agents to do better, but they enjoyed the break from the phones and day to day tasks.

The work environment should be fun:

This is key to happy employees. Start by surveying your employees and ask them what they like and dislike about the office. Ask them if they want anything new at the workplace. Make sure to work towards these improvements to foster a better work environment. Things like, in office cafes and open bars are huge perks that employees love. You don't have to create the Google or Facebook office experience, with slides, hammocks, sleep-pods, etc. Just doing simple changes to the contact center floor can make a huge difference. Adding life size game areas with games like; office basketball and corn hole are always fun. Another great idea is to have a lounge or hangout area. A place that feels like a living room with comfortable couches and a

TV.

Offer career opportunities and employee development:

This shows that you are invested in your employees and are invested in their growth, whether it is internal or external to the team/company. Align them with long term goals and they will be more engaged at work. Giving them clarity into their future opportunities means that they will be open and clear with customers as well. They will want to maintain great customer relations because they know it will benefit the company they are committed to for the long term.

Create a work environment that revolves around leadership:

"Leadership is influence, nothing more, nothing less." - John Maxwell. Agents want to have leaders, not managers. People who they can look up to and learn from. They also want to have the opportunity to lead others. Leaders don't have to have job titles or specific roles, they can be experienced team members or even peers. The secret is to foster an environment that helps this leadership model thrive. If you educate your employees on what leadership really means, they will identify why they are managing instead of leading and start to create more successful teams. Allow them to influence each other in positive ways to create a fun and engaging workplace.

Provide full employee benefits:

It is important to give your employees the benefits they want, not just the ones they need. Yes; healthcare, dental, and vision are important, but don't forget the other valuable benefits. Benefits like; gym memberships, PTO, parking spots, etc. are also huge drivers to employee happiness. Company parties, lunches, and events are great perks that keep employees engaged and looking forward to something. Another engaging benefit is finding webinars, conferences and work events that your employees can attend. For our senior agents and new team leads we send them to conferences and webinars and have them report back any new trends or interesting findings. This is a great way to keep your talented team members engaged.

Celebrate employee milestones:

Make an effort to really celebrate birthdays, work anniversaries, etc. These are important milestones that allows us to feel human as opposed to a number in a system. Every leader should be in charge of writing cards or somehow making these events more than just a "happy birthday." At a previous company we gave the employee the day off if it was their birthday. Then when they came back to work the next day we would have cake and a champagne toast at lunch to celebrate.

Have fun team building events:

Team building doesn't have to be expensive. It's all about the employees. Find out what they like to do and give them an avenue to do it. Don't force them to go to stuffy expensive dinners or company parties. I have found that most of the time the team just wants to go out to lunch or go to a bar for a happy hour. Some of our team members were into video and board games, so we hosted game nights where we ordered pizza and allowed them to use the office common areas. Sometimes just allowing them to change up the scenery helps too. Instead of taking them off of the phones or computers, you can allow them to work from home on a specific day of the year. This allows them to have an enjoyable day, but still be productive and get work done. Or better yet, let them take calls outside the office somewhere. Let them work in a park near the office with a picnic of; food, drinks, and fun activities. All you need is some laptops and mobile Wi-Fi hotspots. You can do this in small groups, so it doesn't create a high IT burden.

Flexible schedules and work from home:

Every employee enjoys the ability to work from home. This doesn't mean you have to allow it all of the time. This can be a benefit or perk you give to employees every once in a while, for a job well done. Flexible work schedules are also amazing perks. Agents love the ability to take a busy weekend or holiday off. I've seen other contact centers incentivizing team members to work a specific shift (in office or during a weekend) by giving them a higher hourly rate. Agents want options. Most of their day is structured and controlled. Agents enjoy feeling that they have the ability to be flexible and have a choice.

Conduct regular performance reviews:

Agents thrive off of feedback. In addition to feedback they like consistency. Regular performance reviews give the team member a sense of where they are in their career and how they are doing at their day to day tasks. I recommend doing annual reviews along with midpoint reviews every 6 months. For one of my teams it was appropriate to do a performance review at the end of their on-boarding (after 3 months in the role). This reassured them that they are doing a good job and are in alignment with the role and team goals. We found that directly after the performance review, even if there was corrective feedback, the agents performed better.

Allow music in the workplace:

As humans, we all enjoy and connect to music. There are studies that say that people who listen to music regularly are generally happier. Other studies state that someone listening to music can do mundane tasks (like drive long distances) for longer amounts of time. Some say that restaurants with music have patrons that stay longer on average and eventually spend more money on things like dessert or coffee, when they normally wouldn't. That is why sit-down restaurants play music and fast food restaurants usually don't. The fast food restaurant wants you in and out. As they aren't in the business of upselling you some dessert after your meal. Music is very personal, this should be encouraged in a way that allows for the agent's personal preference. Some call centers restrict music during working hours due to; distracting productivity, lack of technological capabilities, and/or bias against freedom of noise or expression. I highly recommend allowing music in the contact center and seeing how it can help employees better enjoy their job. Especially in an environment where they don't need to be on phones like; chat or email support.

Treat employees like customers:

We often bend over backwards for our customers and neglect our employees. They are the backbone and voice of our business, yet we often neglect them and rely on them to take the brunt of the burden. I've even heard of the support contact center referred to as the "front lines". This is reference to the front lines in WW1, where soldiers would literally take the biggest force of the opposing army. Why would we treat them like lower or lesser people? Shouldn't we treat them like we treat our customers? If a customer walked onto your call center today, would you treat them the same as you treat your call center agents? Strap a headset on them and make sure they adhered to a schedule. I would hope not. You would welcome them and make them feel at home. That is the same mentality you should take with your employees. Everyone wants to feel welcomed and slightly catered too. This is what will build long lasting engaged employees. Whenever possible, try to treat your employees like you would treat a customer walking in the door.

Think global:

Employees want to be a part of a global company. They want to feel like they have no boundaries and can support every type of issue or customer. This might not be possible in every scenario, but if possible advertise this to your prospective employees.

Map out the employee journey:

We often take the time to map out the customer journey and try to improve it. Often times we neglect the employee journey. Employees go through an employee experience much like a customer. They have a beginning, middle and end. The goal is to design an employee experience that promotes long lasting partnership and engagement into the company and role. Try to focus on those key moments in the employee journey that can define their long-term happiness and success.

Employee metrics and visibility into performance:

Provide your employees with data on their performance. There are performance tools that can help collect and display these metrics to the agents through email or the

CRM. These metrics are helpful to both the agents and leadership. As long as measurable metrics are available and visible, it will create clarity into performance and help employees understand where they are in comparison to their peers.

Create buy-in at every level:

Employees are happier when they have buy-in into the decisions made at a higher level. Bring them into high level decision making brainstorming meetings or allow them to submit ideas for major company changes/initiatives. Even bringing in a couple of call center agents into meetings where new projects or initiatives are discussed, can be very helpful to increasing employee engagement and moral.

Create a senior agent role:

An important part of career path progression is the ability to grow within your job, without changing your day to day role or job. Creating a senior role for contact center agents can help increase employee's engagement and elevate them to the next level in their career. Seniors can also help with leadership tasks like escalations and manager approvals. This empowers the agents along with helping with leadership workload during busy times.

Do external benchmarking:

Look beyond your company to see what makes other companies stand out, with regards to employee experience. Are there competitors or companies in close proximity that offer more to the workforce for working at their company? If so, try to match and diversify yourself to give your company the competitive edge. You don't want to lose your team to another, better employee experience focused company. One of our BPOs in Mexico is located near a major bus stop and this is the differentiator for them to recruit a high level of talent. In Mexico, close proximity to public transportation is extremely valuable to employees. In this example; their location makes them stand out as compared to their competitors.

Enlist C-Level support:

It's important to gain the support of your C-Level. They should be bought-in to investing in your potential human capital. Gaining their buy-in will help you succeed in multiple other areas. I have even seen companies involve C-Level team members in the selection and presentation of quarterly agent performance awards. Employees always respond positively when they see a COO or CEO at one of their call centers. This goes a long way for employees and keeps them invested in the future of the team.

I would be remised to say that the type and age of the workforce you employ doesn't have to do with this strategy. Take into account the age and type of talent you have. Millennials will want different things than Generation X. Wi-Fi in the break rooms and bathrooms may be more valuable than nice photo copiers and free stationary to millennials. Think about the types of employees you want to attract and who are already employed. There are new expectations and ways of supporting employees of a younger or older generation. It's important to keep these factors in mind when thinking about the team and contact center floor.

To truly **Enable Better Service**, you have to embrace the fact that the people on the team have to be happy first. Enabling Better *Employee* Experiences is the foundation to this. Even before talent comes knocking at your door, they look for companies that are listed on the *Best Place to Work* lists. They research your company on Glassdoor and other open and honest company review sites. They search for your brand and look at your website to find out if your company is somewhere they will be happy for the foreseeable future. In today's world, prospective employees get to *shop* around and get much more information about their next potential career job. This creates an environment where all of the best (at least marketed well) companies get and retain the best employee talent. There is more of a separation of upper and lower-class employees due to this new open informational playing field. They might even ask current employees through tools like LinkedIn to get the word of mouth validation of your company before they apply. Word of mouth is a huge influencer into the talent walking through the front door. It's important to market and brand your company through these marketing channels to attract the best talent.

Much like a product, a company's talent pool needs to be nourished and supported. To have the best and most desirable talent on your team you have to focus on; marketing your company environment, supporting learning and development, allowing open and diverse team structure, properly paying and supporting staff, and listening to their feedback. Often times we lose sight of what is most valuable and only focus on selling and supporting a physical product. When the most important asset we have at the company is the human capital sitting in the seats supporting or selling the products we have.

Most companies don't have the resources internally, to the specific department, to create these amazing employee experiences. I recommend leaning on HR team resources to support some of these initiatives, if possible. If not, there are Technology tools out there that you can buy to help support your human capital and increase the quality of the team. Learning, performance, and recruiting managements systems exist to help raise the human capital on the team. These aren't required, but can be useful to help; recruit, retain and develop your most valuable resource... your employees. Even if there isn't enough budget for technology tools like these, I would recommend trying to create more affordable alternatives to help with these areas. Even low-tech Google surveys, docs. etc. can be helpful in kicking off some of these initiatives.

There are 5 key pillars to a positive employee experience. Focusing on these key areas can help prevent turnover and increase the lifetime of your employee base. See figure 15.3 for a matrix on Positive Employee Experiences.

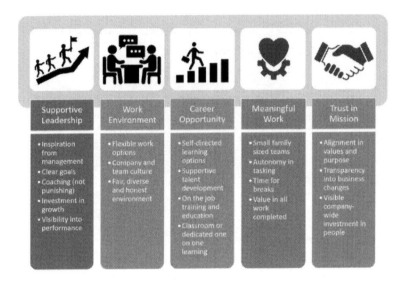

Supportive Leadership	Work Environment	Career Opportunity	Meaningful Work	Trust in Mission
• Inspiration from management • Clear goals • Coaching (not punishing) • Investment in growth • Visibility into performance	• Flexible work options • Company and team culture • Fair, diverse and honest environment	• Self-directed learning options • Supportive talent development • On the job training and education • Classroom or dedicated one on one learning	• Small family sized teams • Autonomy in tasking • Time for breaks • Value in all work completed	• Alignment in values and purpose • Transparency into business changes • Visible company-wide investment in people

Figure 15.3 Positive Employee Experiences

Retention of high performing human capital is extremely important. Recruiting, on-boarding, and training costs make it very costly to backfill an employee. Some estimate it to be in the tens of thousands, depending on the role, area and company requirements. This isn't including the impact it has on the overall team performance when a valuable team player leaves the team. A strong retention strategy is as valuable as a strong recruiting and on-boarding strategy. When thinking of potential costs of backfilling don't forget about the following areas.

- Loss of team productivity while position is unoccupied
- Approval of budget and offer paperwork internally
- Provisioning and internal IT resources for new software and hardware
- Offer perks and on-site travel expenses
- On-boarding training loss of productivity
- Ongoing HR costs supporting the recruiting and on-boarding of the candidate
- Risk of lost time due to candidates declining roles/opportunities

Reducing the potential turnover and increasing the lifetime of your employees is extremely valuable. This is one of the best ways to protect your human capital and increase the overall employee experience. Since backfilling is such a high cost, it is more valuable to create internal programs around retention versus just focusing on recruiting. Potentially getting more return on your investment if you just extend the lifetime of your employees by another year (or even just a month). This not only saves the employees who was potentially leaving but saves the other team members on the team that would have to fill in the gaps while that role is unoccupied.

16

Photocopy your Best Talent – Re-recruit your A Players

We all wish we could take our best agents, take them to the office printer, scan them and make a photocopy. Take your A players, download their brain into a computer and use it to make copies. Sounds like something out of a science fiction movie, but we all have thought about this at some point. Asking questions like, how can I get everyone to be like Megan? What makes her special and how can I get others to be like her? Just wave a magic wand and "poof" a whole team of Megan's.

Unfortunately, this doesn't exist in the real world. We have to hire the best possible talent and train them how to be good at their job. All too often we do this without using true objective or measurable metrics and methodologies. We hire off of gut feel and experience that is listed (honor system of course) on a resume. This is such an inefficient way to find the best potential talent and it often produces less than ideal results. This is quite the opposite of the original goal of making a copy of that A player. What if I told you that there is another way. There is a way to hire new talent that is just like your A players. It isn't a technological tool, it's more of a methodology to apply to your recruiting and training programs.

Start by using what you already have. In previous chapters I mentioned having an Agent Performance Scorecard that can be beneficial for coaching and measuring agents against a common benchmark. You can use that same set of KPIs to find your best agents. Take your best agents and cross reference their backgrounds, previous experience, likes and dislikes, etc., and create an agent persona profile that can help you understand what traits and experiences are good for your team. We did this for our support call center agents in our California location and we found that the best agents came from jobs like; grocery store bag clerks and coffee shop baristas. We then took those same agents (the A players on the floor) and re interviewed them. This time asking them questions like; why do you like your job? Why do you think your good at these tasks? We found that agents who came from these previous experiences are comfortable helping others in a fast pace environment. We discovered that they took a step up (career wise) when they started their support contact center job. Giving them a sense of pride and confidence when they came to work. All of these were factors that helped them with their own personal drive and in the end their happiness in the role.

After realizing that we were on to something, we did the same process but took the bottom performers, agents that were under performers and not an ideal fit for the role. We found that these agents had commonalities as well. Most were highly ambitious and interested in career growth. They had interests in the company and mission but didn't align with the support or customer service vision. Most of these under performers previously came from slightly higher perceived roles and came to work with less confidence or engagement. Roles like managers or team leader in previous companies. No matter what we tried to do for these agents it was never enough to retain them or coach them up and they eventually left. Knowing this information, we created and used a 'positive persona traits matrix' to hire towards. We also designed a negative persona traits matrix to avoid and call out red flags while recruiting. Over time, with this method, we had hired a highly performing and engaged team with almost all A players. Effectively photocopying our A players.

Identifying your A players might be hard. To help with this we created a spider chart that highlighted their Quality and Productivity with regards to specific areas of both. This not only helped us understand their strengths, but also their weaknesses. The filled in area below represents the agent's skill vs. the upper and lower control limit for each area of performance. See figure 16.1 and 16.2 below for examples of a high and low performing spider graphs.

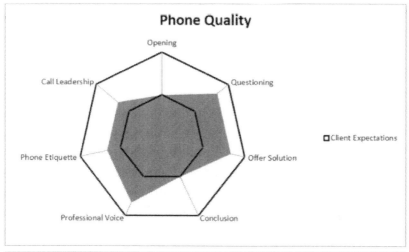

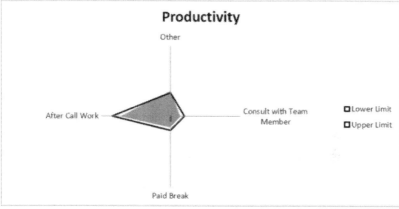

Figure 16.1 Performance Spider Graph Example – High
Performer

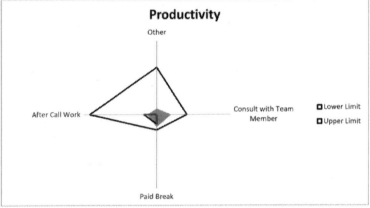

Figure 16.2 Performance Spider Graph Example – Low Performer

The best way to start photocopying your talent is to start with the recruiting process. Here are some best practices when thinking about recruiting A players.

Clear job description and defined role:

When recruiting new agents make sure the job

description is accurate and specific. Include specific skill-based role requirements into the job description instead of generalities. Only ask for what you need, not a general skill like "computer engineering" experience. The more specific and clear you can be, the better.

Skills test and/or live shadowing:

You can simulate scenarios of the job in the interview process to create a proof of concept environment for the new potential employee. This can be in the form of a technical test, on the job shadowing, role playing, etc. Try to mimic the day to day work and apply it to the interview process. For an analyst type role; we put together fake placeholder data and have the prospective team member create visuals and a presentation to show how capable they are in visualizing data. For the contact center; we have interviewees shadow a live agent taking calls, so they can experience what their day to day would be like before they decide to take the job. McDonald's has all of their interviewees work next to the French fry fryers during an interview. This is to test the interviewee to see how they react in one of the harshest environments at any McDonald's location. If they can be comfortable with being next to the fryer, they can handle just about any hard environment at the store.

Structure and plan out all of the details of the interview process:

The key to a successful recruitment process is having a

structured interview process. Make sure each of your interviewers has a clear set of questions that drive to specific types of answers. Craft your list of interviewers and specific questions to unearth specific skills-based questions that pertain to the role. When we wanted to hire technical support team members, we focused on questions that highlighted troubleshooting skills. We even asked them to role play a phone call where they had to troubleshoot a TV remote that wasn't working. Specifically seeing if they asked obvious questions like; is the TV plugged in and does the TV remote have batteries in it. We asked them questions like, how do you solve jigsaw puzzles. Looking for answers with specific details and valuable information. We found that interviewees who started answering that question with questions of their own were the best fits for the role. We found that the most skilled troubleshooter always asks clarifying questions before attempting to giving any answers.

Extend the interview process beyond the new employee start date:

The interview process is often very rushed. With candidates interviewing with less than 5 current employees, it is hard to really assess if they are a great fit for the greater company and team. Even though they are already hired, I would recommend scheduling them 1 on 1 meetings (similar to informal interviews) with other key employees they would be working with regularly. These can take place right after they are hired. We usually setup an additional 30 meetings in their first 30 days that are around 30 minutes long. This allows them to get to know their coworkers/peers and allows existing employees to provide guidance and feedback to the new hire for their onboarding development.

Create a 30/60/90 onboarding plan to recruit towards:

Having a clear understanding of what this new team member will be doing over the first 90 days will help create requirements and a skills list. Mapping out a new hires goals on a matrix or timeline can give the interviewers clear direction into what they are looking for in a candidate. This helps set potential A players up for success, even before they start. See figure 16.3 and 16.4 below for examples of a 30/60/90 Plan and Onboarding Timeline.

	People	Product & Business	Process
30 Days	Schedule and hold 1:1's • 30 x 30 • Additional Extended Meetings with Bond Team Members • Get to know Global Product Stakeholders Org chart (names and roles)	Build knowledge of GMS Product needs • Deep Dive on site, highlight key challenges/opportunities for GMS team members today • Take on first Rapid Response topics/issues	Learn to understand Product process • Where is it working? • What parts are we struggling to implement or follow through? • Identify area(s) for improvement
60 Days	Better understand core competencies of your development team (Product, Development and GMS) • Strengths • Opportunities	Business Acumen • What are short-term goals? How do they relate to Rapid Response? • What aspects of the business are 'weakest'	Meetings & Ceremonies • How does the team like to run their meetings/calls? Is that good? • Which meetings need improvement ? Are we missing any? • Take over Daily Standups & Release planning meeting
90 Days	What are the Bond Team's perceived weaknesses? • Start building an understanding of how the team is perceived • Where do we need to focus on improving partnership? • Stay aligned w/ team on expectations & goals	Begin Developing Product Thought Leadership • What does the product team and engineering see as opportunities? • Begin building a mid-long term plan of product-initiated enhancements	Build Global Partnership Plan • Work with team on an effective partnership approach (meetings, communication lines) • Understand global flow and where its not working well?

Figure 16.3 30/60/90 Plan Example

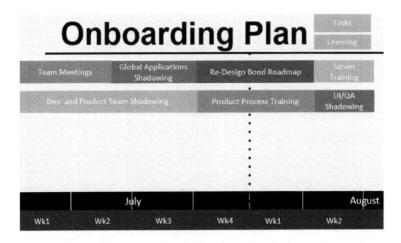

Onboarding Plan

			Tasks
			Learning

| Team Meetings | Global Applications Shadowing | Re-Design Bond Roadmap | Scrum Training |
| Dev. and Product Team Shadowing | | Product Process Training | UI/QA Shadowing |

| July | | | | August | |
| Wk1 | Wk2 | Wk3 | Wk4 | Wk1 | Wk2 |

Figure 16.4 Onboarding Timeline Example

Culturally in the US and Europe a contact center job is not highly regarded. Most agents don't go home for the holidays and boast about how they work in a call center and answer 50+ calls in an 8-hour workday. When I was a front-line agent, I remember going back home for the holidays and getting questions from my uncles, aunts and cousins. They would ask things like; What are you going to do next? Do you really like taking calls all day? I felt like I had to defend my job and highlight how awesome my company/team was. I remember bringing that low confidence and lack of excitement back to me when I returned to work.

For other cultures this is slightly different. Most Asian countries; India, Philippines, etc. actually praise these jobs and roles. Contact center roles are decently paying and stable jobs. In some of these same cultures, they are perceived as a morally good job, as your main role is to help and support others. These agents are bringing back money to support their families and they become key contributors to the family's home infrastructure. This isn't only in Asian cultures, it can also be found in Latin and Central American countries along with countries in Eastern Europe and Africa. These agents usually have natural drive and are honored to work in this environment. It may not fit into your business plans to work with these countries or cultures, but something to always think about when you are recruiting talented and dedicated individuals for your team.

In *Outliers* Malcolm Gladwell talks about the importance of environment to allow performance to thrive. This is what makes the tallest tree grow in a forest. Any seed has the same opportunity as any other. It's the soil, water, nutrients, sun light, lack of herbivore animals nearby that make all of the difference in the small tree's success. What really allows a tree to grow to its fullest potential is the ideal environment? Some of that is luck, but most of it can be controlled. In the contact center your team members are no different. The only difference is that you can control most of the environmental options to set team members up for success. To start, focus on hiring the person that can have the best potential. You wouldn't plant an oak tree and expect it to outgrow a redwood. The same goes for your talent. Recruit key potential A players that can be setup for success. In *Developing the Leader Within You* John C. Maxwell says; "Don't send your ducks to eagle school." This means, let the ducks be ducks and eagles be eagles. If you need a team of eagles, then hire eagles. Don't try to train the ducks to become eagles.

When thinking about who your A players are, you have to focus on more than just the performance metrics. Take environmental factors like seat location on the floor and leadership influence into account. You can have an amazing team member with great potential that is physically sitting next to toxic coworker or under a team leader that is not invested in their career growth. We took performance scores and applied them to a physical heat map of the contact center floor. What we found, not a huge surprise, was that the more productive agents were sitting next to leaders and senior agents. This was because they didn't want to be unproductive in front of their leader and they could use their leader or senior agent as a resource for support in hard situations and professional learning. We found that agents who had little to no line of sight from their leaders or senior coworkers were suffering with their performance. Even if you photocopy your A players, you need to make sure to nurture them with the appropriate environment. The heat map below has an example of this. We anonymized the agents name, but the tenure and performance percentages are real. You can see that the high performers are sitting with other high performers by noticing the high percentages grouped together compared to the low percentages. Work environment plays a part in the agent's success and isn't as random as we would commonly think. See figure 16.5 below for an example of a Performance Heat Map by location on the call center floor.

Jake Brady 1 Year 80%	Francis Berry 2 years 79%	Nina Higgins 3 years 86%	Abraham Harrison 6 months 86%	Eunice Schmidt 5 years 96%	Simon Vargas 6 years 98%
Barry Payne 1 Year 77%	Caleb Gordon 2 years 80%	Blanca Adams 8 months 79%	Opal Guzman 3 years 90%	Vanessa Leonard 4 years 93%	Hubert Fleming 2 years 90%

Kristina Barker 6 months 70%	Steven Rios 2 years 79%	Denise Porter 1 Year 78%	Norma Terry 1 Year 77%	Olivia Reese 4 years 94%	Ivan Ramirez 4 years 98%
Clarence Sandoval 6 years 96%	Sarah Anderson 3 years 89%	Walter Schwartz 2 years 78%	Essie Bush 2 years 86%	Rosie Washington 3 years 88%	Erik Peters 4 years 89%

Alma Hill 1 Year 78%	Adam Becker 3 months 60%	Brandy Howard 1 month 58%	Jan Nelson 1 Year 76%	Jean Larson 5 years 93%	Marcella Lindsey 5 years 97%
Lawrence Alvarado 1 month 63%	Everett Gray 8 months 75%	Tim Tucker 6 months 68%	Clinton Willis 3 months 60%	Pam Garcia 6 months 69%	Raymond Alexander 4 years 94%

Figure 16.5 Performance Heat Map

Notice that there are some high performers that are rather new (2 years tenured) compared to their tenured peers who are under-performing. The team leaders are in the upper right of each row (Simon, Ivan and Marcella).

Another key part to an agent success is training. Instead of using the word training, try using words like educating and learning. Training is usually a negative connotation that is associated to a lower educated animal. For example; you train dogs, you educate humans. Create educational tracks and curriculum that educate your team as opposed to just training them on how to do something correctly. You want a well-educated agent, not a well-trained agent. It is a slight, but subtle difference. Think of the phrase; "Give a man a fish and he will eat for the day. Teach a man to fish and he will never go hungry." Training them to ask for a fish is different than educating them on how to catch fish on their own.

Ongoing education is also an important way to influence the environment and development of your agents. This should be in the form of new hire training and ongoing training. If possible, try to separate your curriculum so that there are advance training tracks in addition to regular certifications. We found that there was success in having a college style grouping of learning curriculums. Team members had *majors* and *electives*. Their *major* should be the job they were hired for, while their *electives* help them diversify their individual proficiencies. I recommend enabling them to learn similar job functions first before learning completely different tasks. Someone in customer service might gravitate to implementation, customer care, administrative, or sales. They might not be as good at marketing, product development, finance, or accounting. This is unique for every company and department. I recommend creating your own career path and educational map specifically designed for your team. See figure 16.6 below for an example of a Career Map.

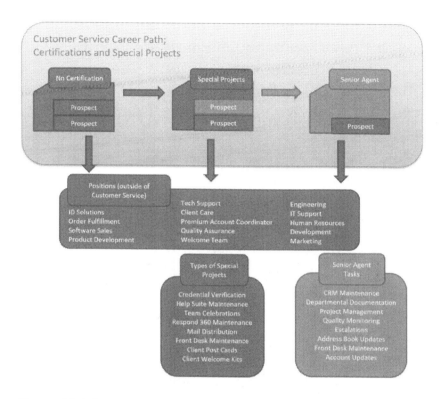

Figure 16.6 Career Map Example

If you really want to photocopy your A players think about giving them the center stage. Since they are the subject matter experts in what they do, leverage them to help create educational material and curriculum for your new hires. They can even be guest speakers in your classroom sessions or create e-learning videos on their own. This will allow your A players to get a rest from the day to day tasks and will help pass down valuable information directly from the subject matter experts.

Tribal knowledge is the secret sauce that every senior A player possesses. It is that information that turns any average agent into a superstar. They possess the tips and tricks, and old history on your company/products as they are within the very fibers of your tenured agents. Tapping into this knowledge bank is extremely important. You never want your team to hold or keep tribal knowledge in, it should be shared between others often. If knowledge transfer isn't done regularly, you might lose the secret sauce from generation to generation of your team. Using internal knowledge base tools can help be a repository for this knowledge. If you are looking for a tool to use, try to find one that has the ability to comment, request edits, and tag employees. This will allow the knowledge to evolve and grow naturally instead of going stale. Once a solid internal knowledge base is established, it can be used as the foundation for a customer facing help-suite. Internal and external knowledge bases usually have similar structure and content.

Create guidelines and ways to identify talent on your team. If there is a measuring stick and open conversation about talent (not to be confused with performance) it can create a healthy work environment. A spectrum from less-talented to talented should be setup and used to measure team members against. Don't forget that this spectrum should be for the current job and potential future jobs. A talented agent doesn't necessarily mean they will be talented as a leader, and vice-versa. Don't just promote your best agents. Instead harness their natural talent and keep them happy and engaged In their current job. Promoting a highly productive agent to become a mediocre leader just waters down both the agent and leadership groups. It also forces the previously high performing agent to learn a new skill set and potentially "start all over". This can be demoralizing to someone who was at the top of the class in their previous role. If you have high performing agents who have a high level of confidence, it's important to keep the agent's confidence with any major job changes. With these tools and techniques, you should be able to photocopy your A players, over and over again.

ACKNOWLEDGEMENTS

This book is a result of a true team effort. I would like to acknowledge the coworkers and people in my life that have helped me throughout the years. This is not only the collective information from peers and colleagues during the writing of this book, but also those throughout my career that have inspired me. Most of the insights provided in this book are from inspirational books, co-workers, leaders, mentors, and other customer service thought industry leaders.

I would like to give a special thanks to my family for allowing me the time to work on this book in my available time. Specifically, to **Alyssa Hinson** for gifting me countless hours to spend writing and doing the final edits to this book. I would not have been able to publish this book without your support. To **Kristin Perl** for being supportive in the curation of this book. Thanks to **Paul Hinson** for reading through the multiple versions and edits while in the draft form, even when on vacation in tropical locations during his retirement. To **Cory Hess** who is inspirational in helping with design and graphic design of the cover and promotional material. For also being the key stake holder in development of all online website material.

To the many managers and leaders in my professional life that have helped me with vision and missions that align with my core moral compass.

Specifically, **Annie Woo** who helped me since my early beginnings in customer service. You are a true inspirational leader and I thank you for your support in my professional education and guidance. To **Anton Von Rueden**, even in the short time we have known each other I can tell we align in vision very closely. You are truly an inspirational leader who knows the importance of developing the leaders on your team to their fullest potential. I can't wait to see how we can continue to partner together and grow. To **Rick Stollmeyer**, you have always been an inspiration to me. You take complex problems and solve them by surrounding them with great people and culture. Indirectly you have taught me that business isn't about making money, that it is more about having fun with your coworkers while getting work done. To **Mike Shay** for your support in this project and dedication to the GMS (Global Member Services) vision. You have taught me so much about vendors and partners, how to scale large customer service organizations, and the importance of celebrating successes. You are one of the most calm and patient leaders I have ever encountered, even in the most stressful of situations.

To the thought leaders who are extremely versed in their respective areas. **Justin Borah** who has been inspirational in the development of the majority of the projects I have completed in recent years. Your dedication to the contact center space is truly amazing. To **Patrick Perl**, your focus and dedication to solving complex problems makes you a thought leader in this space. I am always intrigued to see how you and your team adapts to the obstacles that constantly arise.

To my beloved **Kynsi**, who sat by my side for countless hours while writing this book instead of going on walks to the dog park to play with the other dogs. You are truly man's best friend.

APPENDIX

After-Call Work (ACW)

The Brand Specialist activity that directly follows a call, email, chat, social media or SMS inquiry. ACW encompasses data-entry, activity codes, dispositions, form completion and post-call communication.

Agent

Also known as a telephone/customer service representative (CSR) or Brand Specialist. An agent handles customer interactions and contacts in the call center.

Analytics (Contact Center Analytics)

Using a variety of methods to collect customer data across all platforms in an effort to identify customer needs, increase customer engagement, optimize call center performance and increase customer satisfaction levels. Often used in reference to the visual representation of data driven insights. See business analytics.

Artificial Intelligence (AI)

The ability of a computer to mimic human cognitive skills such as learning and understanding.

Automatic Call Distributor (ACD)

A specialized phone system used for handling incoming calls. The ACD recognizes an incoming call and scans for predetermined identifying information. This Information is cross-referenced against a database of call routing instructions and distributes the call accordingly.

Automatic Number Identification (ANI)

A protocol for providing phone number information to a receiving phone system, such as an automatic call distributor (ACD). ANI essentially functions as caller ID, often delivered via tonal frequencies carried over the phone line.

Average Handle Time (AHT)

A key performance indicator, AHT measures the average length of an interaction, including hold time, talk time and after-call work.

Average Speed of Answer (ASA)

Metric used to calculate the average time a call remains in the queue until a Brand Specialist has picked it up. This is sometimes called average delay.

Average Talk Time (ATT)

Normally expressed in minutes and seconds, this measures the time spent speaking with a customer. It is one component of average handle time (AHT).

Business Process Outsourcing (BPO)

Contracting a business function, such as finance, human resources or contact center services, to a third-party provider.

Call Center

An operation combining human, technical and physical resources to field inbound and/or place outbound phone calls. Call centers support a number of different industries and functions, and often handle contacts via channels beyond the telephone, including email, chat, social media and SMS. Call centers deploy technological solutions and operational processes to distribute contacts to teams of Brand Specialists, often located in one or more locations. Also see contact center.

Call Center Forecasting

Calculations based on rigorous mathematics and experience that are used to predict call volume. The expected volume is in turn used to project the required staffing in the given time. Many different factors can affect the forecast, including seasonality, marketing, promotions and organic brand growth.

Call Center Service Level

Can refer generally to agreed-upon levels of service in either an outsourced or internal call center environment. The term service level also commonly refers to the specific metric measuring the percentage of calls answered within a predetermined time threshold.

For example, an 80/20 service level refers to a target of 80 percent of inbound calls being answered within 20 seconds.

Caller ID

Displays a caller's information on the telephone or on a separately attached screen. This allows the receiving end to identify who is trying to contact them. Important to consider company branding on outbound calls.

Channel

Paths of communication, such as phone, email, chat and social media. In retail, it can also be used to define delivery method.

Chat

Like an instant message system, this allows any logged-in computer Brand Specialist and customer to have a written conversation online and in real-time.

Chat Bot

A computer program that replicates conversation via internet messaging, sometimes used in e-commerce, call centers and customer service as a virtual agent to provide information on a limited topic.

Coaching

The process of optimizing Brand Specialists and

program performance through positive reinforcement and encouragement. Conducted in conjunction with call monitoring and quality assurance evaluation sheets to assist in identifying opportunities for improvement.

Command Center

A group within a call center program that has responsibility for such workforce management functions as real-time schedule adherence, agent skilling, scheduling, forecasting and reporting.

Contact Center

Usually synonymous with call center. A contact center will handle email, chat, social media, SMS and faxes – not just calls. The International Customer Management Institute (ICMI) defines a contact center as a coordinated system of people, processes, technologies and strategies that provides access to information, resources and expertise, through appropriate channels of communication, enabling interactions that create value for the customer and organization.

Cost Per Call

A metric used by calculating the total cost of running a call center divided by the number of calls handled in a given period.

Customer-centric

A business strategy that is concentrated on the

customer's needs and satisfaction.

Customer Effort Score (CES)

A customer satisfaction survey used to measure the degree of effort the customer felt they had to expend to resolve their issue. The second version of the survey asks the customer to agree or disagree to the statement that the organization made it easy for them to handle their issue. The first version of CES asks the customer to rate the amount of effort they had to put forth to handle their request.

Customer Experience (CX)

The culmination of a brand interaction. The specific outcome and the corresponding emotional reaction that results from a customer's interaction with a Brand Specialist. The goal of a Brand Specialist is to satisfy customers and go beyond, creating experiences in which customers feel that their well-being is the top priority for both the Brand Specialist and the brand.

Customer Journey

The total of all experiences a customer has during their interactions with a company or Brand, as opposed to the experience from one contact for a single transaction.

Customer Journey Mapping

Graphically depicting the story of the customer's

entire experience with an organization that identifies key interactions and discusses the customer's feelings and motivation. A customer journey map helps the organization learn about its customer and provides insight into gaps in the experience that can be used to improve the process.

Customer Lifetime Value (LTV)

A company's revenue or profit from transactions with a customer over the lifetime of the relationship.

Customer Loyalty

One of three levels of value in the call center, providing distinguished service that improves customer retention and transforms customers into advocates, according to the International Customer Management Institute. The other two levels are efficiency and strategic value.

Customer Relationship Management (CRM)

The strategy of identifying customer needs, improving customer interactions and customizing contacts, sales approaches and automation to provide optimum service to each type of customer to maximize the bottom line benefits to the organization. It is a broad term that takes into account people, processes and technology related to the acquisition and retention of customers, and the maximization of the value of each customer relationship.

Customer Satisfaction

The degree to which a customer feels their expectations have been fulfilled by a company's products and services.

Customer Satisfaction Score (CSAT)

Represents customer satisfaction. CSAT, used to calibrate the product delivered against the customer's anticipation for the product, is expressed as a percentage with 100 percent reflecting complete customer satisfaction. There can be a large discrepancy between the CSAT scores of companies even within the same industry. When comparing scores, it is necessary to investigate the process in which the scores and benchmarks are assigned.

Customer Service

Working on behalf of and for the satisfaction of a customer.

Efficiency

Using resources in the most cost-effective manner. One of three levels of value in the call center, according to the International Customer Management Institute.

Email

Messages distributed by electronic means from

one computer user to one or more recipients.

Erlang

A unit of measure used in telecommunications to denote the optimal traffic capacity or load in a given service element, such as a circuit or a switch. Expressed in terms of time, assuming no call blockage due to uneven arrival patterns, a capacity of one Erlang equates to 60 minutes of traffic per hour; as arrival pattern complexity increases, blocking theory comes into play, and additional service elements will be required to ensure optimal call distribution (see Erlang models, Erlang-Engset).

Facebook

A social media platform where friends, families and co-workers can connect. Direct posts on one's page can only be made and received by Facebook friends, facilitating more privacy than on Twitter. Common platform for enterprise social media customer care. See social media customer care.

First Contact Resolution (FCR)

Properly diagnosing and resolving the customer's issues on the initial point of contact. This customer relationship metric illustrates the quality of service customers are receiving by measuring how often their issues are resolved on the first point of contact. Typically supported with a CRM or Case Management application.

Full-Time Equivalent (FTE)

A full-time equivalent equals one employee working full-time. The formula to determine the number of FTE positions required for a specific program: Total FTEs equals total number of scheduled work hours divided by number of hours one full time person will work per week. For instance, a program that requires 800 scheduled work hours a week and a 40-hour fulltime work week will require 20 full-time equivalent Brand Specialists. (800/40=20). An FTE calculation can also take into account staffing situations in which the combined weekly work hours of several part-time people equal the hours of a full-time person.

Handle Time

The time a Brand Specialist spends taking a call, doing after-call work, handling any necessary and extraneous details, and the time it takes for the technology to process the work.

Idle Time

Time that is not spent on a call or doing after-call work. Expressed as a percentage of logged in time.

Inbound

Incoming calls, emails, chats, social media or SMS inquiries that are initiated by customers and prospects.

Interactive Voice Response (IVR)

An automated retrieval and processing device that provides information to callers via telephone keypad signaling and/or voice recognition. The response may be a recorded, artificial or synthesized voice. Common applications include bank by phone, check on my order and store locator.

Job Description

A written summary of the role and duties of a specific position. The description may include information such as job title, purpose, responsibilities, tasks, working conditions and designated supervisors.

Key Performance Indicator (KPI)

Calibrates performance of an organization through the monitoring and analysis of integral metrics.

Knowledge Management System

In relation to handling customer interactions, this system maintains a database of relevant knowledge used to assist the Brand Specialist when providing information to a caller such as product information, cost, warranty, company policies, installation, usage and maintenance.

Lifetime Value (LTV)

A company's revenue or profit from transactions with a customer over the lifetime of the relationship.

Live Chat

Like an instant message system, this allows Brand Specialists and customers to have a written conversation online and in real-time.

Mission Statement

A broad, general statement that declares an organization's aim and how it will go about achieving it.

Monitoring

The process of observing and evaluating calls, emails, chats and social media interactions in an effort for program management to quantify and score the way a Brand Specialist represents the brand, listens to the customer and assesses the steps needed to assist the caller, and whether the desired result was achieved by the end of the call.

Multichannel

A market strategy that uses multiple independent channels to reach a customer, such as brick-and-mortar, catalog, or website.

Net Promoter Score

NPS is a leading growth indicator based on a survey that asks customers how likely they are to recommend a brand to friends and colleagues, on a scale of 0 to 10. The respondents are divided into three categories: promoters, who score 9-10 and are loyal enthusiasts; passives, who score 7-8 and are satisfied but unenthusiastic; and detractors, who score 0-6 and are unhappy customers who can damage reputation and growth with negativity. NPS equals the percentage of promoters minus the percentage of detractors. The score can range from -100 to 100.

Occupancy

The percentage of time a Brand Specialist is logged in and available to accept incoming calls, email, chat, social media and SMS inquiries or other tasks versus the time that they are logged in and idle, waiting for the next interaction. This calculation can be obtained by dividing workload hours by staff hours.

Offered Call

Offered calls are those received by the automatic call distributor (ACD), whether they have been answered or abandoned. It is important to note how your organization or outsourcing partner is specifically counting offered calls. Some may start at the switch level, before the call reaches a recorded message and others may start the count after. Note that in the latter case, blocked calls or busies may not be counted.

Omnichannel

An extension of the multichannel approach, emphasizing the synergies across all channels for an enhanced shopping and customer care experience whether the customer is shopping online from a personal computer or mobile device, by telephone, or in a store. For example, a customer can purchase an item online and then pick it up at the brick-and-mortar location.

Onboarding

The process of bringing a new employee, client or customer into the folds of a company, by showing them the ropes of their job, the culture of the company or the way a company works in partnership with its clients. Onboarding may involve formal orientation and training, or a series of events designed to bring the personnel up to speed and able to work as part of the relevant team.

Outbound

Contacts made by Brand Specialists to reach customers and prospects. Includes calls, emails and chats. The opposite of inbound.

Outsourced Call Center

A partnered, external institution that handles all or some aspects of the customer service experience, which may include interactions by phone, email, chat, social media and SMS on behalf of a company or organization.

Outsourcing

Contracting with an outside company to handle some or all of an organization's contacts with customers and prospects.

Pooling Principle

The principle states that movement toward consolidating resources results in improved traffic-related efficiency. Conversely, moving away from resource consolidation results in reduced traffic-related efficiency.

Procurement

The act of acquiring or buying goods or services from an external source, often by a bidding process.

QA Evaluation Sheets

Forms used for quality assurance monitoring and assessment of Brand Specialist interactions with customers. The forms provide a performance checklist that is both a guide for Brand Specialists and for the individual evaluating them.

Quality Assurance

The activities put in place by a company or organization to ensure that the quality requirements for a product or service are achieved.

Quality Analyst

An employee or consultant with responsibility for reviewing processes and procedures of a company.

Quality Monitoring

The process of reviewing calls, emails, chats, social media and SMS inquiries and screen activity to make sure that all processes and production meet standards and the brand message is being presented properly. Brand Specialists can be monitored or from a remote location.

Queue

Sequencing process where a call, email, chat, social media or SMS inquiry is held until a Brand Specialist is available to accept the interaction.

Random Call Arrivals

The manner in which a call center receives calls, not based on any kind of pattern or interval system.

Real-Time Adherence

Measures the degree to which a Brand Specialist performs to the work schedule planned for them. The automatic call distributor (ACD) can display real-time statistics to convey the current state of a Brand Specialist. Adherence is determined by comparing a Brand Specialist's active state to his or her schedule.

Real-Time Management

In response to current queue conditions, making adjustments to staffing and thresholds in the systems and network.

Received Calls

Calls that are received and taken by a trunk, which can either be answered by a Brand Specialist or abandoned.

Recruiter

An employee with responsibility for hiring staff by collecting and evaluating resumes, conducting interviews, completing background checks and recommending qualified candidates.

Remote Agent

An agent who works outside of the contact center. He or she is usually connected via telecommunications links that provide voice and data pathways. The agent can work on a fixed full-time schedule or on an as-needed basis.

Request for Proposal (RFP)

A request made by an organization for a supplier of a service to submit a business proposal outlining its costs and capabilities. The subjects may include company background, core competencies, references, recruiting, training, workforce management, technology, telecom, data security and the business continuity plan.

Response Time

The time it takes to respond to a request for

service. Response time can refer to contacts that don't have to be handled immediately, such as email, and can be expressed as follows: 99 percent of contacts handled within X minutes or hours.

Retention Rate, Customer

The percentage of customers who remain customers over a specified period of time. A related term is save rate, which is the percentage of customers over a specified period of time who called to cancel their service, subscription or membership, but decided to remain a customer after speaking with a Brand Specialist.

Retention Rate, Employee

The percentage of employees who remain with a company during a specified time. The Society for Human Resource Management provides the following formula to calculate retention rate: Number of employees employed for entire measurement period divided by number of employees at start of measurement period multiplied by 100. Also see, attrition rate and turnover.

Schedule

The specified time an employee is required to clock in, or be on duty, to handle contacts. The assigned days and hours an employee works.

Schedule Adherence

How well an employee complies with his or her

scheduled work times, including start, stop, break and time off.

Screen Pop

The delivery of corresponding data associated with an incoming call that is presented on a computer screen, provided by interactive voice response (IVR), automatic number integration (ANI) and computer telephony integration (CTI) technology.

Seasonality

Fluctuation in the volume of business from one-time period to another. These changes are often predictable from past experience and are dependent on the nature of an organization.

Segmentation

Compartmentalizing customer contacts into various categories, dependent upon such factors as value or relation. Each category can configure an appropriate treatment.

Self-Service

The ability of a customer to serve themselves guided by a company system such as interactive voice response (IVR) or an internet website.

Service Level

Conveyed as the speed of answer, service level

accounts for the percentage of calls to be answered within a specified number of seconds. Often reflected as a percentage.

Service Level Agreement

An interdependent agreement entered into by two or more organizations that defines which aspects of services will be provided by each party.

Short message service (SMS)

An electronic communication transmitted and received by cellular phone. Text messaging. See text.

Shrinkage

The paid time that staff is not available to take calls, expressed as a percentage. Factored into staffing requirements, shrinkage accounts for breaks, meetings, training, off-phone activities and paid leave, among other things, allowing sufficient staff to be scheduled to meet service goals.

Skill-Based Routing

Rather than using the first available Brand Specialist, skill-based routing transfers a call to a Brand Specialist or group of Brand Specialists that are considered to be the best at handling the specific needs of a caller.

Skilling

The act of monitoring contact center queues and redirecting Brand Specialists to queues with calling and email volume spikes as needed.

Social Network

Internet-based media platforms that facilitate intercommunication and are geared toward staying in touch with people virtually rather than physically in the area. Other uses include brand promotions, common interests and social movements.

Speech Analytics

Recording and analyzing calls, often using speech-recognition software, in an effort to better understand the needs of the customer, evaluate the knowledge and skill set of your Brand Specialists and to optimize customer interactions.

Speed Of Answer

The time a caller is waiting to be connected with a Brand Specialist. Service level and average speed of answer (ASA) are both factors in speed of answer.

Supervisor

The person that typically has first-line responsibility for the management of a group of Brand Specialists. Responsibilities may include monitoring, measuring performance, coaching, assisting with difficult or escalated calls, training and scheduling tasks.

Talk Time

The time between when a Brand Specialist answers a call and when they disconnect.

Tech Support (Technical Support/Help Desk)

Assisting the customer in resolving a range of technological issues, such as troubleshooting technology and/or maintenance of software systems in an effort to resume continuity and maximize technical performance.

Telecommuting

Communicating by telephone and/or a computer system to perform job duties from off company premises without traveling to and from a main office.

Text

An electronic communication transmitted and received by cellular phone. See SMS.

Ticketing System

A system to record or document interactions with customers. A ticket is created for each caller to include all the information concerning the transaction. The ticket can be created and resolved or escalated. The same ticket number remains with the same incident to allow for easy access to information for subsequent discussions or actions. Tickets are maintained in a case management or CRM system.

Unavailable Time

The times in which a Brand Specialist is not able to take or make calls. Breaks, lunches and corollary time for managing and processing administrative work are all components of unavailable time.

Universal Agent

A Brand Specialist who can process several different types of contacts and can usually oversee any type of call, offer advice and aid in the handling of a variety of customer concerns.

Virtual Agents

An online animated character that, using artificial intelligence, holds conversations with customers to assist them with customer service and other questions.

Visible Queue

When a caller is informed by an automated announcement about an expected wait time. This allows a caller to choose to wait, abandon a call, or request a callback.

Voice of the Customer (VOC)

The aggregate evaluation of the customer's needs and expectations, which can be gauged through feedback from customers, customer service representatives or by listening to call recordings.

Voice Over Internet Protocol (VoIP)

A system that is able to transmit telephone data to the internet, thus making the internet a source of communication in the same way that a telephone is. This facilitates callers to bypass the telephone entirely and use a free network to make long-distance calls.

Warm Transfer

When a Brand Specialist talks to a caller, but then escalates the call to another Brand Specialist or supervisor for further assistance. The smooth transition of the transfer is orchestrated through efforts such as telling the caller to whom they'll be transferred and apprising the new Brand Specialist or supervisor of the caller's name and the details of the interaction.

Workforce Management (WFM)

A contact center discipline that uses historical information, future forecasts, contact channel volumes, interaction durations and schedules to determine an optimal staffing for a given time period.

Workforce Management System

A system charged with the tasks of creating staff schedules, determining staff requirements, forecasting calls and tracking performance of Brand Specialists. This system is automated, thus severely reducing the time and cost of hiring employees to do this manually.

Workforce Optimization

The science of using the workforce as efficiently as possible at the time when it is needed.

Workload

The combination of time on a call and the work done after a call. It can include the combination of ring time, delay time and conversation time. It may be applied to either Brand Specialist requirements or infrastructure planning requirements.

Wrap-Up Codes

Brand Specialists enter codes into the automatic call distributor (ACD) in an effort to ascertain what type of calls they are handling. Reports can be generated by call types, handing time and time of day.

Wrap-Up Time

Consists solely of the time that Brand Specialists spend doing after-call work. This does not include meetings or breaks.

Source: https://www.globalresponse.com/resource-center/the-call-center-glossary/

ABOUT THE AUTHOR

Ever since 2008 Aarde Cosseboom's professional experience has been in the contact center world, helping service businesses and consumers through cloud-based SaaS (Software as a Service) products and technology. He enjoys working with large global customer service teams to increase and leverage the following areas of business; leadership, customer experience, customer success, operations, technology, customer service, recruiting, and people development.

He is an entrepreneur at heart and has a knack for business, starting and owning small businesses across multiple different verticals. Some of his past businesses include; online retail ecommerce, online membership subscription wine ecommerce, and contact center technology consulting.

Aarde is a thought leader for many customer service and contact center organizations and often speaks at conferences about people, process and technology. Speaking at CCW, ICMI, IQPC, VentureBeat, Frost & Sullivan and many other conferences regularly. He belongs to the NICE InContact ICVC (InContact Visionary Council) and NUG (NICE User Group). He has won multiple awards; 2018 NICE InContact CX Excellence Award for Best Cloud Implementation, 2018 NICE InContact EU Interactions Award for Cloud Excellence, 2014 Voice of the Customer MOJO Award, and was a finalist for 2014 ICMI's Global Call Center Best Use of Technology Award.

Aarde has partnered with key leaders in the industry to design and develop complex technology tools to include; Chatbots, Virtual Voice Assistants, Socialbots, CRM/IVR integrations, Machine Learning for customer segmentation, custom Smart and *Bullseye routing* techniques, and caller identification tools.

Aarde enjoys traveling and exploring the uniqueness of how the world works. Always eager and interested in learning and adapting to the world and its unique complexities. He enjoys working with complex global business needs and isn't shy of solving issues for large and complex businesses.

For the majority of his adult life he has lived in the central coast of California in the town of San Luis Obispo. He recently relocated to Los Angeles in 2016. While in San Luis Obispo he attended Cal Poly San Luis Obispo studying Industrial Engineering and worked at a local SaaS (Software as a Service) provider called MINDBODY Inc. Aarde was fortunate in being involved at the Senior Leadership level for MINDBODY Inc while they went IPO in June of 2015.

To learn more about Aarde and find out where he is today follow him on his LinkedIn here - https://www.linkedin.com/in/aarde-cosseboom-99755546/

If you are interested in learning more about contact center technology and partners visit https://www.goclariti.com to request more information.

Made in the USA
San Bernardino, CA
15 April 2019